CW00482298

*"In recent years we've all h
the things we take for gro
were taken from you ai
approach a second chanc
help us all see the world dif*
– Matt Brittin, Presi

*"This is such a humbling and inspiring read. I've known
Matt for thirty years, and his story is phenomenal. In this
book he's given us a fantastic lesson in how to live life to
the full and make the most of every day."*
– Katie Derham, BBC Radio 3 Presenter

*"This is an extraordinary story – close to a miracle!
Matthew is my brother-in-law, so I've watched his story
unfold from close quarters. He played a catalytic role in
Alpha becoming a course for those outside of the church.
This is a fascinating account of his recovery from a near-
death experience and the different perspective and
insights this has given."*
– Nicky Gumbel, Pioneer of Alpha

*"Matthew is the very epitome of endurance, courage and
resilience, but his greatest achievement has been
learning not to take anything for granted and for being
eternally grateful on a daily basis. We can all learn an
enormous amount from his extraordinary personal story."*
– Jon Ridgeon, CEO World Athletics

SECOND CHANCE

Making the most of all that life has to offer.

PublishU Ltd

www.PublishU.com

Thanks

I'm thankful to so many people. I pray you'll forgive me for pulling out only a few names here. I'm especially grateful to the Lord, who told me to marry the most important person in my life: Samantha. I can't thank Sam enough, nor do justice to the love, care and consideration she's shown me over the first thirty years of our marriage — especially over these last seven, very trying years. Thank you, my darling.

Thank you also to my four wonderful children: Max, Bear, Bean and Haz, along with my parents, Colin and Janet Smith. I hope I've provided a sufficient level of entertainment and value throughout my life so far.

I further thank my friends, many of whom are also work colleagues, who've journeyed through life with me — be that a few short steps or a much longer segment of the journey. You've all played a significant role in shaping me and my life to this point. Let's keep connected and see what the future holds.

A special thanks to Erik, Jonathan and Michael for your understanding and patience with me, as you've helped me pull this book together. Finally, to Mum, taking me back to the late seventies and checking my "homework!" You were always very good with "their" or "there" and commas, to allow the reader to draw breath. Nice to know you've still "got it," in your eighties!

Contents

Introduction

This story is to encourage you, the reader, a) to live your life in a way that enables you to make the most of every moment and b) to make a choice *now* about Jesus Christ.

The single, most important question, that everyone has to answer, whether they want to or not, is: "Was Jesus who He claimed to be?"

We all know we're going to die one day and on that day the answer we've each given to this question will have a more significant impact on us than anything else in our lives, ever.

Life up until this moment, the moment of death, is a constant stream of choices that we each have to make. How we make those choices and what we decide has a significant impact on ourselves, those closest to us and potentially those much more loosely connected with us. These are the opportunities in life and working out how to make the most of each and every opportunity is a great challenge. For most of us, this challenge is aided by working together, learning from each other and helping each other to live life well.

I don't want to end up in eternity knowing I could have been clearer about what I've learnt from nearly dying in 2016 and miraculously not only surviving, but being restored to full health. There was so much in life that I'd taken for granted, wasn't appreciating or making the most of and it's such a waste. I don't take any second for granted now. I'm not saying you must believe what I believe, but I implore you to consciously make the choice yourself as to what you believe about Jesus, a simple Yes or No. Was he the Son of God, who died for your sins on a cross and was raised back to life after 3 days?

Enjoy everything and every single moment. Life is a precious gift — make the most of it!

Matthew

SECOND CHANCE

What I'd really like is for every reader of this book to consciously make a decision about Jesus Christ and what His death on the cross means for them.

Chapter 1

Setting the Scene

"'What shall I do, then, with Jesus who is called the Messiah?' Pilate asked."

- Matthew 27:22

The alarm went off. I got to it before the second ring; already awake as usual. I pulled myself out of bed and headed downstairs to make a bowl of porridge and to get ready. It was before 07:00 and a regular Saturday morning in May in the UK. It wasn't raining, the temperature was comfortable in the mid-sixties, overcast. I'd be on the bike by 07:30; fuelled and ready to ride. I'd be meeting up with the other Frodsham Wheelers for our regular Saturday morning ride out to the Wizard Cafe in Alderley Edge.

That's usually what happened on a Saturday morning. This Saturday on 21 May 2016 however, changed everything for me. Instead of arriving back at home later that morning, having had a few very enjoyable hours of exercise, my next conscious memory occurred when we were nearing the end of July. I'd been technically dead for a few minutes. As a country we'd voted to leave the EU, our prime minister David Cameron had stepped down and everything, especially for me, felt totally different. I was lying in a corner bed within a large room with seven other beds in it and a wide range of different people in them. Surprisingly, it didn't feel weird. It just didn't feel quite normal. I remember feeling quite content — not anxious or disturbed. I just wasn't connected with what was going on around me at any level.

I've asked my wife Sam, to give her version of events:

"The night before the accident, Matthew said that he'd had chest pains but thought he'd only pulled a muscle. I tried to persuade him to go to the doctor, but he said he was too busy. He was under a lot of work stress and cycling was his way of coping. He did agree to go if he wasn't feeling well in the morning. That morning when I woke up and realised Matthew had gone cycling, I thought he must've felt better. I'd taken the kids to the garden centre to buy a few plants for the garden. As I opened the front door I heard the phone ringing. I ran to answer it. It was the police who called to say that Matthew had been in a bike accident and had been airlifted to Stoke hospital.

I rang our neighbours and they kindly agreed to look after our two younger children Beanie and Harry. As I drove to Stoke, I felt pretty helpless and cried out to God. I felt Him say 'you can pray and get others to pray too.'

When I got to Stoke, I was taken to a side room and they said that Matthew had had a cardiac arrest and that it had taken somewhere between seven and twelve minutes to restart his heart. He would have had significant hypoxia (i.e. lack of oxygen to the brain) and that I should get all family members to the hospital as soon as possible. They further explained that he'd be put in an induced coma on a ventilator.

I made the phone calls, barely able to speak through my tears. I remembered again what God had said about praying, so I made a WhatsApp group of Christian friends I trusted to pray for Matthew. Over the next few weeks, the knowledge that this group were praying, not just for Matthew but for our family, gave me so much peace. I've always believed that it's good to pray specially for things and I'd post the latest thing the doctors were concerned about. If any of you are reading this: Thank you, kind friends, for your prayers! Another friend organised a prayer evening. Thank you! As Matthew was brought out of the coma, even though he had amnesia and it was weeks before he started to make new memories, he had his sense of humour and I thought 'We're going to be OK.' For those who don't know (I certainly didn't), 'retrograde amnesia' means being unable to remember things from before the injury and 'anterograde amnesia' affects the ability to make new memories. Matthew had both. This meant we could tell him he was in hospital and he had had a bike accident and then ask him where he was and he would just look blank and say, 'I don't know.'

Slowly Matthew recovered over the next few months."

It's only now as I'm writing this, nearly seven years later, that I'm still measurably changing (hopefully some might say improving), every sixteen to twenty weeks and the experiences of these last seven years are the reason for writing this book. The last six months have, surprisingly, been the hardest and some of the reality of my situation and of life is really beginning to strike home. We're all different, we have different strengths and weaknesses, but we're created to "do life" together. We all love and are loved, each of us have needs and wants and the capacity to give and receive; to support and tear down. We're all going to die. Do you even think about your own death? What legacy will you leave? What will be written about you? Do you care? Should you care?

I will not be holding back in the book about my Christian faith and whilst I'd love you, the reader, to be sharing this faith with me, that's not what this book is about. This book is about the choices we make.

Life is a gift — we get to do with it what we want. The aim of this book is to help you, the reader, make the best choices for you and the life you want to live.

I'm certainly not trying to tell anyone how I think they should live their lives: One of the joys of life is the freedom we've all be given to make our own choices, however challenging that might be for some. This book is to share with you the lessons that I've been given the opportunity to go through, because of my cardiac arrest whilst out cycling, the subsequent brain injury and the slow journey back to some semblance of normality.

The most important decision in life is our decision to either believe that Jesus Christ is who He claimed to be — the son of God who died so that we could be reunited with the Lord for eternity — or to not believe in Jesus Christ. I strongly, as strongly as I possibly can, encourage you to make this decision. Don't wait and don't procrastinate; make it, because it's fundamental to what will happen to you when you die.

What shocked me, and was one of my first thoughts lying in that hospital bed once I had an idea of what had happened to me, was that I very nearly died. That death can come out of the blue and if it came out of the blue for some of my mates, there was a chance that they hadn't accepted the gift Jesus wanted to give them. They were getting on with life, putting off making a decision that can easily appear too big for some, or unnecessary for others, which I see as effectively meaning that they were choosing "no" — they weren't accepting what Jesus did for them. So, whilst it might feel like not making a decision and not being sure/just putting it off, effectively it had exactly the same effect as deliberately choosing not to believe. I don't want anyone, especially my mates, to not realise that they're either in or out and the only way to be in, is to accept what Jesus' death on the cross gives us.

I believe, with every cell of my being, that the Lord is real. I cover why I believe this in much more detail later in the book, but what I'd really like is for every reader of this book to consciously make a decision about Jesus Christ and what His death on the cross means for them. As you'll see, if you read on, some of the people that have impressed and helped me most over the last six years, have been confirmed atheists, which whilst I find it difficult to understand their decision, I totally respect them for having thought about it and made a decision. It's the joy of the freedom we have, just like it's the joy of the life we have, to decide to do it our own way.

Hopefully this book will help you with those decisions you face every day and make it easier for you to make the most of every moment and every gift you've been given.

The second main reason for writing this book is to help you to make the best decisions you can, in your life, for you, for your family, for those closest to you and also for everyone else in the world. This can seem like an ideal that's unobtainable and therefore not worth even trying to achieve. I'm now of the opinion that it's relatively simple and we're the ones that make it confusing, complicated and hard. I've found, through necessity and with help from the Lord, a way of navigating decisions that before I'd have found much more troubling, as I weighed up various conflicting elements to each one.

I also feel it would be helpful to let you know a little bit about me. I'd just turned forty-nine when my cardiac arrest happened. I'm married to Sam and we celebrated thirty years of marriage in August 2023. We've been blessed with four wonderful children (Max, Claudia, Antonia and Harry) and we live in the Northwest of Britain. I've always loved sport but was very lacking in talent when a ball was involved. Fortunately, I was quite tall at 193cm and had the opportunity to get in a boat at school, eventually ending up in the boat race for Cambridge in the late eighties, along with doing some J18 and U23 representation for the GB team. I studied Economics at Cambridge University and went on to qualify as an accountant with Price Waterhouse in London. At this stage in my life (I was a non-Christian), I didn't not believe, I simply didn't bother to think about it. I had what I thought were more important things to do with my time, than go to church. I just didn't see going to church as relevant to my life. It was at this stage that my best friend at university, Erik, who was a committed Christian and had invited me to countless events over our three years at university, (most of which I'd attended relatively happily and none of which had made much of an impact on what I felt was my pretty amazing life) didn't give up and asked me if I'd be interested in doing an Alpha course. He cleverly didn't sell it that way. He knew I was taking the district line tube home every evening, that it passed through South Kensington and he offered me food, a chance to catch up with him and meet pretty girls every week for ten weeks. I'll leave it with you to decide which of the three was most appealing, but as a single guy living alone for the first time and learning to fend for myself, I can tell you that two of them were measurably more appealing than the third! What did I have to lose? It was towards the end of this course when I was faced with making my decision. This was effectively forced upon me by another friend from university who, in relatively blunt terms, told me to stop being an "*****" and to make a decision. I listened to the arguments, had my questions answered and then needed to stop being an idiot, to either truly accept who Jesus was and what He'd done for us or to reject it and walk away properly. I'm not sure, to this day, whether I'd have made a clear decision about what I believed, if I hadn't been pushed like I was. Looking back, I'd now say that that is often how God works, but I was fortunate to be told what I needed to hear at the time. I'l be forever thankful to this person for pushing me in the way she did, because I believe that the Lord will never do anything more to individually call us to Himself, but He will be and show Himself to be exactly who He is: our loving, caring, consistent Father in heaven, as well as our Creator God.

I decided there and then that it was highly likely to be true, rather than untrue, so I said to myself that I'd take that step and publicly declare what I now believed: that I believed that Jesus was God's Son, that He was born to a woman, that He lived a sinless life and was put to death on a cross; that His death allowed our perfect God, our Father in heaven, to accept us as righteous, because Jesus' death had paid the price for our sins — all of them. At the time it theoretically made sense and over the last thirty years it has practically made sense. When I had the cardiac arrest, pretty much everything of Matthew was stripped away and that stripping-away allowed me, actually forced me, to turn to the Lord for help. It wasn't the help I thought I wanted, because I didn't have a clue what I wanted or needed, but the help the Lord could provide. It's this help that has been transformational and that I really want to share with you. Most of it could be described as "common sense," but as I think we all know, common sense isn't always so common and it's the application of it when everything appears to be falling apart, that's so difficult.

I had no idea what I wanted to do after university. I knew I wanted to keep rowing, so London was the obvious destination and I knew I needed to earn money to pay for living. That was about it. Different companies were going around Cambridge encouraging students to apply to work for them and this was often a good source of food, so I happened to be at one evening event hosted by Price Waterhouse (PW) and was talking to someone there that was interested in rowing. He persuaded me to come for an interview the next day. I duly went along, was put through their interview programme, and was offered a job with them that would see me qualify as a chartered accountant.

I started working in London, at PW's office, Southwark Towers, just above London Bridge station, living in Chiswick, rowing out of Tideway Scullers. I duly qualified, and got the opportunity to work for PW in Lisbon, Portugal for six months, which coincided with getting married to Sam. I'd describe it as an ideal start to married life: A new country, new friends, new work colleagues that I could get to know with my "new" wife. Perfect. On returning to London, still with PW, I worked on a number of projects around the privatisation of the Regional Electricity Companies and became aware that climbing the ladder in a firm like Price Waterhouse, wasn't my idea of an ideal career, so I started looking around and ended up in a corporate finance department at BOC, mainly looking at proposals from around the world to invest in gas plants. This was based outside of London, so I got a taste of commuting and working for a big corporate at the same time.

It was during this time that our first baby was born, July 1995, at the Chelsea and Westminster Hospital. Everything was going smoothly until this baby appeared and he was coughing. He had Strep B and was put immediately on a ventilator. It was horrible and I felt totally powerless and totally responsible at the same time. Sam and I couldn't pick him up, there didn't seem to be any part of him not affected by tubes and medical devices and we couldn't even stroke or really touch him. Max pulled through, but the experience left Sam and me thinking more deeply about what was really important in life.

It was early in 1996 that Mum and Dad and their business partner Alastair Barker had decided to try and sell the small business they'd founded in 1974. This business, Texkimp Ltd., had been started in my bedroom at home, forcing Dad to not only complete the work on a house he'd bought in Knutsford, Cheshire, so that I could have a room upstairs, but to start up a business in the textile machinery sector. This was a sector that he knew well, as he'd been running a family business that Bill Kimpton, Mum's father and my grandfather, had founded — making machines for processing fibres, mainly for customers in the UK. I've virtually no personal knowledge here but have been told that the problems that led to that business being sold in the late sixties, were predominately twofold: Firstly, it was the decline in the manufacturing of textiles in the UK and secondly, union pressures making a UK manufacturing company barely viable. This led to that business being sold on to a larger engineering group, with my father working for them for five years.

However, I believe that both these factors had a significant impact on how my parents decided to run Texkimp and this was based upon two main strands: Selling globally and using subcontractors for all (or virtually all) of our manufacturing. The idea was that if it was possible to contract with someone to do a job for you, at a competitive price and quality, then by following this approach, the business could be run at a very low-fixed cost base, making it more resilient to dealing with the peaks and troughs of machinery manufacturing. They'd stuck to this approach and in the early nineties, whilst having survived nearly twenty years, the pressure was telling and my father was feeling most of it. Alastair, their business partner, whom my father had met whilst studying engineering at university, was a few years older and they decided that the best course of action was to sell the business. This would allow Alastair to step away and pursue his passion for vintage cars and my parents to have sufficient money to allow my father to take a reduced role in either Texkimp or another business.

It was March and Sam and I were planning to drive up from London that weekend with our young baby to celebrate with Mum and Dad that they could step away from the pressure of the business, when I received a call from Mum telling us not to bother: They'd gone to the final meeting to sign the papers, when the acquiring company had informed them that they'd had a change of mind and that they felt the business was only worth a lower sum. I'm certain they still wanted it, but they saw a vendor with no other options and thought they could get a better deal. They hadn't read my father very well. Apparently he asked them if they were serious, and when they said they were, he packed up his papers and left the room. When the purchasers asked when he was coming back, they were informed by my mother and Alastair that he wouldn't be back and that the deal was off. My father refused to sell the business to people that he had shaken hands on a deal with, who then in turn tried to get the better of him.

We drove up to Cheshire. Somehow, today I'm sure it was the Lord's will, I ended up saying "What about me?" and Sam and I agreed that we'd come up north to take on the business. We bought Alastair out at the agreed price and got on with running it. I cover a little of the business story in a later chapter, but this was a key step for us. Due to me being a non-engineer and not very practical, Sam still does most of our DIY as she's far more capable and politely keeps me out of the way. Here we were joining my parents in a very small, engineering business they'd started; the second generation of a family. I wish I'd known then what I know now — about really, practically walking through life with our Lord, rather than trying to do it in my own strength.

People tried to empathise with me by explaining how they also struggled with the very things I told them about.

Chapter 2

Waking Up

"Wake up! Strengthen what remains and is about to die, for I have found your deeds unfinished in the sight of My God."

- Revelation 3:2

It was weird, but at the same time absolutely fine. I was in a hospital ward, there were eight beds and I was in the far-right corner as you walked into the ward from the other end. I have absolutely no recollection of my time in intensive care. This was the rehab stage and whilst I think it was now clear that I'd live, there was a real uncertainty as to how well my brain was functioning at that point and would function in the future. I just remember taking everything that was going on at face value. I was recognising my family (sort of), but what had happened was in the summer of 2016 and my last memories were just before 2010 and these were sketchy.

I've since concluded that I'd lost one hundred percent of my memory back to 2010, about eighty percent back to 2000 and along with it, improving the further back I went in time. This meant that the '70s up to the mid-'80s, things were clearer than they had been just before the incident. It was as if the weight of new memories had squashed the old ones down and now that that weight had been lifted, the old memories filled the space again. What was even more interesting was what (smells, sounds, tastes, textures) triggered a connection with a memory in there. I was told, and believed it to be true, that I hadn't lost my memories, I'd just lost the connections to them. Therefore, different stimuluses would reconnect memories. The challenge then was keeping the connection that I'd just remade, as my short-term memory was diabolical.

I also struggled with things that had changed culturally over that period, which was effectively anything from six to twenty years depending on the memory loss. These changes in circumstances normally happen gradually over time, so one becomes accustomed to the change slowly and you hardly notice it, if at all. For me, a few changes felt so significant that it was hard to process them rationally and react in the appropriate way and even after seven years, I needed to be consciously aware of certain things being the norm now and consciously how I needed to react.

Probably one of the most significant changes and one that I know is so unimportant that I can comfortably write it here, is beards! "Beards?" you might say. Yes, beards! In what remained of my memory, men generally wouldn't have beards or facial hair — especially in the upper ranks of businesses and in positions where the presentation to the public was key. This had then changed and there were some well-known people sporting beards. In earlier years, generally beards and facial hair were uncommon and when it was present, it was well groomed. When I woke up in 2016 it felt like facial hair and ungroomed facial hair was on nearly every male face. I've got nothing against facial hair, apart from envy (as one who couldn't ever grow anything worth keeping). I was aware that this facial hair created a reaction in me that needed to be overcome, to ensure I treated everyone equally. It also served as a reminder to me that I was out of step, out of kilter, with the rest of society.

In this rehab situation, there were others who were recovering from various accidents and it was a supportive and safe environment. I have a few very strong memories from those days: One in particular was my inability to make a decision and the fear that that created. When I was asked whether I'd like a cup of tea or a cup of coffee, I was unable to answer. How did I know what was right? I knew I liked tea and I liked coffee, but how did I know which one to choose? I didn't, so I couldn't. However, if I'd been asked a simple question that required a yes/no answer, this was generally OK, so I could answer the question. "Would you like a cup of tea?" with a simple yes or no — no need to choose. This rapidly started to improve, however still today, making a decision with multiple inputs that are changing, can be very challenging. I'm learning how to best deal with it but have a real appreciation for how people recovering from a head injury need both the understanding of the people around them that the recovery can take a very long time and secondly that their personal level of performance can vary markedly, due to the circumstances of the moment.

I was given much advice, but one piece that has proved invaluable from those early days, that I still refer to on a regular basis, is that to manage my situation I needed to understand my levels. This is both very simple and phenomenally deep. If you've never had personal experience of a head injury, but are interested in understanding more, then pay real attention here. I know that most head injuries and those suffering from them are different and we will all feel and react in different ways, so it's important for each person to be treated as an individual. However, I believe that managing our levels as a principle, is key to everyone (brain injury or none): We just learn from a very early age in life how to do this sufficiently well enough to cope, with living, most of the time.

What I was taught, in my very limited state, was to think of myself as having three boxes that were connected but separate. These three boxes were a) Physical b) Mental and c) Emotional. I was then told to learn to measure two things: Firstly, "how full" each box was and secondly at "what rate" was I filling up each box. If any of the boxes got completely full, I'd cease to function and as I neared capacity in any box, I'd slow down. Now I'm sure that most of us have a good feeling for our physical state: we know how tired we are, we know how hard we can push ourselves and for how long, before we collapse. A good example being that you'd know how fast you could try and cover a hundred metres and how fast you could cover the twenty-six miles of a marathon. We would all need to go slower for the longer distance. Mentally, a lot of us have also learnt how to pace ourselves: We know how long we can productively study for, how fast we can write in an exam, how long it would take us to answer certain types of questions, etc. We'd all be different (just as we're different physically), but we'd all have a fair appreciation of how mentally tired or fresh we were and at what pace we could operate.

However, the third box, the emotional box, was a complete eye-opener. Maybe this is just me — a fifty year old, British male being expected to understand his emotional state and his emotional level of output. I could easily be reduced to a shell of what I'd been only a few moments earlier. This could happen with virtually no warning and with my lack of awareness, would catch me out. What it meant practically was that I was then unable to properly process what was going on, I became unable to make sensible decisions and therefore struggled personally, but even moreso, I think it became difficult to have me around, because the emotional element that had tipped me over, was generally not seen or felt by anyone else. Therefore, I just appeared irrational and unstable.

I don't know if this next comment is just me or if other brain injury survivors have felt something similar, but generally, we as a human race seem to think that people get comfort from empathy and therefore I felt a significant number of people tried to empathise with me by explaining how they also struggled with the very things I told them about. Now I'm certain that everyone was well meaning and trying to be helpful and some might have dealt with much more serious brain injuries than I had, but personally I wanted understanding, not always acceptance of what I was unable to do or cope with. I didn't want to be treated differently, but I knew I had to be. I didn't want exceptions to be made for me — I'd have preferred to be held to the same standards as everyone else and then be forgiven after I'd failed, rather than before I'd tried. Potentially one day, I'll understand more about how other people have felt and coped with the recovery from their brain injuries. I know it was very interesting seeing the world I thought I knew, through a different lens.

The memory loss was fascinating and I really mean this. Whilst it could have been concerning and worrying, it wasn't — it was just different. I think this was harder for everyone around me; the fact that I couldn't remember and was repeatedly surprised by how things had changed. The bits that have stuck with me are around the key bits of my life. My children had all grown up and changed significantly, my parents had also changed measurably and when I finally got out of the rehab unit, what I found was wonderful. But getting out, was a full production in and of itself.

Before the medical staff were happy to sign me off, I was made to perform an errand that gave confidence that I could survive by myself. This task was to go and buy some food and cook a meal. Fortunately, Mum had taught me to cook as a child and I'd had to cook decent meals for myself for quite a few years, especially while I was rowing. So, I knew how to make a meal. However, to get to the supermarket to buy the food, I needed to catch a bus. This was a new experience and I can still feel the uncertainty of getting on a bus, paying for the trip, knowing when to get off and then how to catch the bus back. At the end, the bus trip felt like a real achievement, but I think this might have been the case without the brain injury! The supermarket was a slightly different event, because there was such a big increase in the choice available, over what I remembered.

I knew what I wanted. I'd decided to make a spaghetti bolognese and knew the ingredients, but there was so much in the shop and buying only what I needed was challenging, as everything was packaged in certain sizes and I didn't need as much as I was having to buy. I did manage to get it all within my budget and get the right bus back, very relieved when it stopped on the road outside the building that I thankfully recognised as the rehab unit. Preparation of the food was also interesting and if I'd been aware, it would have been a big indicator of the challenges to come. I'd met other patients and was allowed to work with them in the small kitchen area that we had. One guy who I'd become friendly with (let's call him John), was very willing to help and we decided that we'd prepare this meal together for the two of us. Now I knew how I would cook the spaghetti bolognese, how I'd been taught by Mum all those years ago and those memories were fresh and strong. What I didn't have was the awareness that working with someone else would be so challenging. John also thought he knew what to do and he had his own struggles, so neither of us was willing, or probably able, to understand the others position and perspective. We both wanted to get the job done, but it had to be done the way we both wanted to do it. We got around it and ended up cooking what I thought was a great spaghetti bolognese, but I can still remember the feeling in the kitchen of John wanting to go about the cooking in a different way from me and me only wanting to do it the way I knew: I had no flexibility or even ability to understand what mattered and what was of no importance.

Having ticked the box to "get out" as I saw it, the day of escape arrived. It wasn't as if I was even really interested in getting out and home (there was so much about life that was taking my attention), but getting home was just the next big step I'd been told I needed to take. Sam arrived and we put what limited stuff I had in the car and drove off. Everything was great, until I realised that I had no idea where she was taking me. We had moved since 2010 and I had no memory of where we now lived, the house we ended up in, that Sam told me was home, "felt right" but that was it. I had zero recollection of ever moving there or living there.

Over the next few years, I learnt to trust that "felt right" or "didn't feel right" sensation. It wasn't a hundred percent guarantee, but it was enough to cause me to stop and question where I was or what was going on. One of the things I'd been told about the memory loss, was that I probably hadn't lost the memories, but I'd just lost the connection to them. I think this has been very accurate and recreating those connections was done by way of many different things (often not what you'd expect). I found that smells, colours, tastes, textures and some sounds caused memories to come back, sometimes very sharply and quite often they were memories that were completely irrelevant to everything going on around me. One in particular stands out: The shape of a blade of grass and how it felt between my fingers. I was lying on the grass under a rowing boat, somewhere in the world, which was all I knew. A few weeks and quite a few phone-calls later, I tracked it down to a rowing event in the eighties but am pretty certain that I hadn't ever thought or recalled that memory ever before. Why would I? Why would I remember something so insignificant? It was the start of an appreciation of how amazing our brains are, how much information they are potentially storing that we have no idea about and how the important thing might not be remembering something but learning to connect to the memory that's already been fixed in there. Learning how to use the tools that we individually have to achieve what we individually need to achieve is, in my opinion, far more important than learning "how to do something," from someone else who naturally wants to teach you to do it their way. We are, at the same time, so very different yet so very similar.

Chapter 3

The Event

"For all have sinned and fall short of the glory of God and all are justified freely by His grace through the redemption that came by Christ Jesus."

- Romans 3:23-24

The alarm went off at 06:15, but I was awake as usual, just lying in bed looking forward to the day. I've always been a morning person, I love being with people and taking exercise is one of my passions, so Saturday morning was a treat. I even felt I was being a good example to the family, not lying around, but looking after myself, getting on with things, other than work.

So, the dog "Liebe," a large Münsterländer, was quickly let out into the garden, the porridge was put on and I went to check my bike over. Much to my wife's probable distress (I'd never asked and I don't think she'd say), I had turned our potentially beautiful dining room into my man cave; it was just the most convenient room for storing all my bikes and bike stuff, a Concept2 rowing machine and some weights. It also happened to be near the front door with some nice views out of the window.

Fuelled up and with my kit on, I headed out to meet up with the Frodsham Wheelers and our regular Saturday morning run on the bikes out to the Wizard Cafe in Alderley Edge. It's a great run, just over 100km that takes us out and back through the lanes of Cheshire, passing through Knutsford where I grew up and is my perfect start to the weekend. I've always found that getting on a bike is very similar to getting in a boat: You can leave every care in the world behind and be solely focused on what you're doing, who you're with, how your body is performing and the conditions you're operating in. If any of those nagging thoughts creep in, it's a simple matter of turning the pedals harder, pulling the oar harder, using the increased effort to completely block them out, blissful, even if it hurts physically. This Saturday, it was the usual pit stop at the Wizard and then the ride back. On the return journey it was usual for groups to be breaking off as individual members would try themselves against the route and others and afterwards Roy's comment to me was that he knew something wasn't right, as I didn't usually keep him company towards the back of the pack. Fortunately for me, I had his company alongside as we cycled along Toft Road into Knutsford and apparently, I just keeled over into the middle of the road. Fortunately for me there wasn't a car close and the car driving towards me, was being driven by a hospital anaesthetist, Adam Dobson, who was off to play golf with his son. Adam says that he saw the way I fell and knew it wasn't a cycling incident, stopping immediately. It was the combination of Adam's experience, medically but also in pressured situations, along with the paramedic, Roy and the other Frodsham Wheelers with me, that saved my life. I'd had a cardiac arrest, caused by a bit of cholesterol that had built up in my artery, breaking off and blocking the artery in my heart. When the heart stops, the blood stops pumping around my body and when the brain stops getting a fresh supply of oxygen, life is precariously balanced.

I asked Adam and Roy to share in their own words what happened that morning:

Adam Dobson

"A quick Saturday morning trip to the golf driving range with my ten-year-old son Arun was what was planned. The weather was grey and threatening rain, so it seemed an ideal way to pass an enjoyable and leisurely morning.

Assuring my wife Helen that we wouldn't be too long and that there would be plenty of time for the myriad weekend chores to be done on our return, we set off. Our house is situated on the outskirts of leafy Knutsford, on the main A50 towards Holmes Chapel.

Soon after setting off, on the outskirts of town not far from Toft church, whilst in the midst of educating Arun on how to achieve the perfect golf swing (from a twenty-four handicap golfer), I vaguely noticed a fairly large peloton of cyclists heading at speed in the opposite direction into town, a fairly common sight in flat and rural mid-Cheshire.

One of the cyclists suddenly appeared to lose control of the front wheel of his bike and crashed sickeningly head-first into the tarmac.

As a Consultant Anaesthetist with life support skills, two thoughts immediately flashed through my mind. The first was that I had relatively little time for an enjoyable morning with my son before a long list of tedious domestic jobs to attend to, and the second, which gratifyingly won out on the day, was that this incident looked more than a simple tumble off a bike and that I should go and offer assistance.

I pulled over to the side of the road, with the sky turning a dark grey threatening heavy rain, and assured Arun that I wouldn't be long.

On running back, I found a disquieting scene. The cyclist was lying motionless on his front, with his cycling colleagues milling around in an evident state of distress and uncertainty as to what to do. A quick assessment revealed that he was unconscious, wasn't breathing and had no pulse.

My gentle morning's golfing had taken an unexpected and fairly dramatic turn.

Working in a large acute city hospital I'm fairly used to managing teams in crisis situations and it was clear that this was a crisis. With help, I quickly and carefully got our casualty over onto his back so that we could assess him more thoroughly – he remained unconscious, and it was clear that life support was needed. The rest of the peloton at this stage were marshalling and halting traffic on this busy 'A' road. I later found out that the ambulance was called by a friend heading back into Knutsford to pick up his car after dining with us the night before who had got caught in the ever-expanding tail-back of traffic!

On request, one of the other cyclists showed willing in starting chest compressions, and with some brief instruction from myself, applied himself to the task admirably. I knew I had a portable 'Laerdal' face mask in a medical kit in my car. With evident extensive trauma and lots of blood on the face of this complete stranger, mouth-to-mouth resuscitation without some interface between us was not something I felt comfortable with. I rapidly retrieved the medical kit from the boot of my car and managed with some difficulty to establish an airway to ventilate and oxygenate our patient, whilst at the same time directing and reassuring my non-medical chest-compressing assistant of the brilliant and essential job he was doing.

Our life support efforts continued until, after what seemed an age but in reality, was only a matter of a few minutes, a paramedic in a fully equipped rapid response vehicle arrived. By this stage torrential rain had started, and I was aware that the phone in my pocket was ringing repeatedly. Clearly my wife had heard the sirens, seen the stationary traffic backing up outside our house and assumed that her husband and son had been involved in a terrible accident! I was in no position to respond at this stage as I was updating my very welcome paramedic colleague with details of the situation and applying cardiac monitoring, whilst continuing with providing life support. We already knew that we had a cardiac arrest situation, but the monitor revealed that with DC defibrillation (electric shock) we could try to restart the heart. Three shocks and a dose of adrenaline later, the heart restarted, and our patient started to make some effort to breath.

He was still unresponsive, but we now had signs of life.

On arriving at the scene, the paramedic had immediately realised the gravity of the situation, and that a large field was immediately adjacent to where the events were unfolding. He had the presence of mind to call in the air-ambulance, which arrived shortly after the successful defibrillation of our patient.

My phone continued urgently ringing, the rain continued falling and my son continued waiting patiently in the car for his dad! Clearly, golf was off the agenda for today.

I was now in a position to hand over ongoing management to the incredibly talented paramedic and air-ambulance team, and within less than twenty minutes from the arrival of the helicopter we had our patient scooped up and off to the major Trauma Centre in Stoke.

Then I answered the phone (as expected it was a very anxious wife) and went to retrieve my somewhat bemused son from the car where he'd been patiently sitting for the last forty-five minutes getting wet: his window was open, I'd got the keys and the heavens had opened during all the goings on: he didn't want to come and disturb me!

After a thorough debrief in the back of an ambulance with the police and paramedics (as well as a much-needed mug of tea from an extremely kind lady from a nearby house who provided refreshments to practically everyone involved), I headed home to relate the events that had occurred. My initial reflections were a certain satisfaction at recognising and dealing with a traumatic situation and managing the available resources at my disposal, with an outcome that, under the circumstances, was as good as could have been hoped for. I was extremely thankful for the timely arrival of incredible support and somewhat in awe and proud of a health system that, although flawed and frequently criticised, could mobilise so effectively and so rapidly to remove our casualty to a centre of excellence for, what I hoped would be life-saving treatment.

I then went about my day. A protective mechanism that I'm sure I share with many of my colleagues in front-line medicine in coping with the everyday stress of traumatic events such as this, is that, once I've dealt with the situation in a professional and competent manner, I don't dwell on it. I have the ability to remain somewhat emotionally removed. This is an attribute that I have always felt is essential to do the job effectively. Accordingly, I then went about my day as planned, concerned for the well-being of my cyclist-patient and medically curious as to how events had transpired.

Over the next few days information started to filter through regarding the identity of the unknown cyclist, who I had no expectation of ever seeing again. His name was Matthew Kimpton-Smith: a life most definitely worth saving!"

Roy Forster

"We started from the pee stop. We were on the route out to the Wizard at a steady pace. Matthew was complaining about feeling rough and aching and wasn't well. We went out through Knutsford, past the Esso service station and continued out to the Wizard Cafe in Alderley Edge. We had regular breakfast stuff — it was a regular Saturday thing. He had been cycling for quite a while, getting stronger all the time. On the way back the group usually played a little: someone would accelerate and others would try and keep with them or do leap-frogging, etc. This Saturday, Matthew was on a long stretch back into Knutsford (everyone was going for it). Usually Matthew was at the front; this time he was at the back and so I said 'Keep up, what's up with you?' I thought I'd jump on his wheel and keep up and a couple of seconds later he went down. Christ what's happened there? I stopped, turned the bike around and he was on the floor, bleeding with his glasses in his mouth; choking. I pulled the glasses out of his mouth. When I got no response from him, I checked for a pulse: nothing. The rest of the group had returned. There was a field next to us. Matthew was removed from his bike. No cars were behind us. We were right in the middle of the lane. I was a basic first aider at work (INEOS Runcorn and could operate a defibrillator and give oxygen). Matthew was choking on his glasses, but when I removed them he was still choking. He wasn't breathing properly; he was choking and making a rasping, gasping noise. I started CPR and was fortunately carrying a mask *under my seat. It wasn't a great scene. Adam arrived and put something down Matthew's throat. At that point, I had no idea that he was a medic but was relieved that he appeared to know what he was doing. I started CPR and chest compressions, focusing on "do your best, try and don't worry."*

Time appeared to fly with Adam arriving, but it was a good while until the helicopter landed and the paramedics arrived in what I think were two ambulances. The road was shut while all this was happening.

The rest of the cyclers just watched, unable to do anything more. We picked up all the plastic bits that had fallen into the road. A local lady gave us a sugary drink and offered to help. Matthew was loaded into the helicopter and with Chris Hanson-Jones we cycled Matthew's bike back home."

Everything is so much easier in hindsight, but in reality, with cars building up on the road wanting to be on their way, an unresponsive body of a mate, and the CPR breaking bones in my chest, it would have been so easy to stop and wonder what the right thing to do was. However, seconds count and it's because of the quick response and clear thinking in the moment, that I'm able to be writing this now. Other members of the Wheelers were dispatched to get help and I ended up with an air ambulance landing in the adjacent field, the defibrillator restarting my heart and a quick flight to the hospital in Stoke. I fortunately don't remember any of this. Actually, I don't remember any of my rides with the Frodsham Wheelers.

I was flown to hospital and spent the next couple of weeks in intensive care. Sam was called and was advised to also get the older kids back from wherever they were, as it certainly wasn't certain that I'd survive. Max (20) our eldest was at university in Durham, Claudia (19) was out in Chile on her Gap Year working with Latin Link, and was flown home. I meanwhile was the only one not aware of anything going on, being well cared for in the Intensive Care Unit (ICU) at Stoke.

SECOND CHANCE

They introduced me to others as "Matthew — the out-of-hospital cardiac arrest patient." After this had happened a few times I asked why they said it as it felt odd. The response was that it wasn't usual to have an out-of-hospital cardiac arrest patient able to walk around and function as I was functioning.

Chapter 4

Playing the Game

"Rejoice always, pray continually, give thanks in all circumstances; for this is God's will for you in Christ Jesus."

- 1 Thessalonians 5:16-18

"Indeed the very hairs of your head are all numbered. Don't be afraid; you're worth more than many sparrows."

- Luke 12:7

While in Rhosneigr, the reality hit me. It was chaos and I was chaotic; everything wasn't right. It wasn't that it was wrong, it just wasn't right and there was so much to process, that I couldn't cope. In losing so many years of memory, not only had things changed in that time, but there were also cultural shifts, things that change slowly and are totally accepted because it's just what happens. However, I found that these cultural shifts, happening in a big jump, were harder to deal with than factual changes.

A good example of what I'd call a factual change, is that a child would be five to ten years older than I remembered them to be, so the way they looked and acted was significantly different. People would have done work on their properties, so the property would be different. People had got divorced, some had remarried, had moved to a different house in the village. All changes that needed to be assimilated, but were fairly easy to understand.

Cultural shifts however have been much harder to fully assimilate and have taken work to do it. The best example is "beards," which I've covered in chapter two on "Waking up." The kids are fairly rude about the facial hair I managed in hospital. I've not quite decided whether Sam was right to not let them take a picture — it could have been entertaining, now that I'm nearly back to some sense of normality.

We all make numerous decisions every hour when we're awake and each one of these has an impact on ourselves and those around us. Like a rock or a pebble being thrown into water, the ripples can be tiny and barely noticeable or huge and have a big impact.

Some of you might be keen golfers, some might play sporadically and others might never have swung a club. Hopefully you all know something about the game, but if not, the aim is to hit a small white ball around a course. The course consists of eighteen holes, each of which is a stretch of earth, ranging from approximately seventy-five metres to seven hundred metres, from a tee box to a putting green. The aim is to hit the golf ball from the tee box into a hole in the green, with as few number of shots as possible. You play each hole on the course, eighteen for a full round and add up the total number of shots you've taken to hit your ball from the tee box into the hole for each of the eighteen. The winner is the person who takes the fewest number of shots. Each hole is designed to be played in anything from three to five shots and when the total number of shots that all the eighteen holes are designed to be played in, are added up, that is called the "PAR" for the course. This is usually around seventy-two for most courses. So, if you take seventy-two shots, you go around in PAR. Most golfers aren't good enough to do this, so there's a handicap system, giving them shots on the harder holes, to try and make the game fairer for all levels of player.

The Lord said to me, "You're not a golfer Matthew, but you understand the concept of PAR and I want you to play life to PAR." At this point I had no idea what He was getting at, but being so switched off and in a just existing state, I just filed it away, over the next few months it became obvious that playing life to PAR, meant having the right Perspective, the right Appreciation and basing every decision on the fact that our Lord is Real. Living like this, is living life to PAR, as the Lord designed it to be lived. If I was just told this, or reading it without the experience I've had, I'd immediately start thinking that we're all different, we all have different circumstances and therefore different reasons to do things differently. I'm now of the opinion that whilst this is true, the Lord has designed life to be lived in a certain way and whilst it will be different for us all, we're all called to live it in a very similar way. Unfortunately, through pride, isolation and events, we've adapted and justified what and how we live, so much so that we each have our different norms and preferences for how we want to live. What I'm finding is that when I step off the treadmill of living and re-evaluate what the Lord has told me, it makes so much sense and covers many of the issues that we're seeing in the world. The next few chapters are going to cover in more detail what living with the right Perspective on life and the right Appreciation of life are like, alongside recognising that the Lord is a Real Creator God, who knows each of us intimately. Ultimately, I believe we're called to work together, whether that's countries working together to steward our planet or neighbours in a street working together to help each other — we're called to be in all sorts of relationships.

My head was still in a mess and I needed to keep everything simple. Now that I've had nearly seven years of recuperation and healing, still measurably changing every twelve to sixteen weeks if I behave, I'm starting to understand things like why my healing has been taking the time it has. I know, 100% know, that the Lord could've healed me instantly, but He didn't. He's healed me at the right pace for me and how He wants to use me. There are many people that He doesn't heal and I'm sure there are many readers of this book asking why someone they know, or even they themselves haven't been healed. We cover this a little more later in the book, but the Lord knows each and every one of us intimately. We don't have any say in that. We can try and hide as much as we like, but it has no effect. However, in His love, grace, and wisdom, He's given us free will and that wouldn't be the case if He withdrew it in certain situations. This free will has led to great successes in the world, but also terrible disasters. This free will is what makes us who we are and with it comes the responsibility to decide whether we want to enter into a relationship with our Heavenly Father, or not. He's waiting, with open arms, to embrace us as His children, He's doing this, already knowing all the bad stuff that each of us tries to keep hidden, buried in us, but we have to make that choice. Not making it; not making a decision whether to enter into such a relationship is, exactly the same as choosing to not enter into the relationship. Why? Because we have to step into our

Father's arms. He's not going to pull us in — we have to step in and welcome His embrace.

So here I am now, seven years later, mentally significantly improved: not needing to sleep during the day and able to involve myself in normal activities for prolonged periods of time. Whilst this is great, it's made me realise that "life" is coming back to what I'd call normal, people around me are seeing me as "normal," but it's made it significantly more difficult to live, as I believe the Lord is calling me (potentially us), to live. They introduced me to others as "Matthew — the out-of-hospital cardiac arrest patient." After this had happened a few times I asked why they said it as it felt odd. The response was that it wasn't usual to have an out-of-hospital cardiac arrest patient able to walk around and function as I was functioning.

I'll cover this in the next chapter, but relationships are about time and our time is finite. We have twenty-four hours in every day, each hour has sixty minutes, and each minute has sixty seconds. We achieve things by using our time in the right way and we only achieve good relationships by using time well. What the Lord's been teaching me over the seven years of steady recovery, is that how I decide to use my time matters. The world around me will make demands on me, there will be expectations from the society within which I live, of how I use my time. The important thing is that I realise how I use my time and make wise decisions with it.

He kept the instructions to live life to PAR simple, because that's the best way for them to be followed and have an impact. When I was at an early stage of recovery, understanding and living to PAR was relatively simple. Straightforward Perspective on life, easy and strong

Appreciation for the very basics, like moving and breathing and a simple knowing that my Father God was Real (just like my earthly parents are real). I know that Mum and Dad, Janet and Colin, are there for me. If I pick up the phone, they'll answer it. If I knock on their door, they'll welcome me in. It's just the same with my Heavenly Father — I know He is truly Real.

Now, as I'm nearly back to living normally, I have to stop and make sure that my mind is straight, that I'm making decisions in the right way, for the right reasons. Life is much more confusing and having the ability to simply and easily take a step back and tick off the 3 boxes of P, A and R, makes living so much easier and I believe the outcome of everyday is better for me and others affected by my decisions.

SECOND CHANCE

*The Lord told me that
life was all about relationships.*

Chapter 5

My Tower

"Turning around, Jesus saw them following and asked, 'What do you want?'"

- John 1:38

"'For I know the plans I have for you,' declares the Lord, 'plans to prosper you and not to harm you; plans to give you hope and a future. Then you will call on Me and come and pray to Me and I will listen to you. You will seek Me and find Me when you seek Me with all your heart. I will be found by you,' declares the Lord."

- Jeremiah 29:11

In what I'd describe as my feeble attempts to pray, I think I was actually just starting to really communicate with our Lord: gone were my ideas as to what God should be doing. I was really trying to talk to Him but more importantly, to listen to Him. The Lord gave me what I've termed "My Tower" — a very simple way of making decisions that I struggled with through fear.

The Lord told me that life was all about relationships. These are the primary bits to life and I should view them as a tower. At the top of this tower was my relationship with Him, the Lord, and everything I did in life had to be either something that enhanced my relationship with Him or at worst have no effect on my relationship with Him. I could do nothing that would have any negative effect on the relationship I had with the Lord. Remember, He is all seeing and knowing — so no getting away with anything!

Next down in the tower was my relationship with Sam, my wife, and everything I did with Sam had to either enhance my relationship with her or at worst be neutral to that relationship, but this relationship was under the relationship I had with the Lord, so everything had to be pleasing or neutral to Him. The next level of relationship was with my children and again, everything I did with them had to either enhance that relationship or at worst be neutral and had to comply with the rules for the relationships above. Now I felt the first pang of guilt, because I knew that I could say things to the kids, that I thought helped them, but I might not have said it if Sam had been listening. Below the kids, there was a level of wider family, then it was friends, then work colleagues and the tower continued to grow in height and width. The same rules applied at every level.

Relationships are so important. As I investigated this, I found a growing body of research indicating that we are profoundly relational creatures and it pushes away the notion of a self-made self. We are formed by and dependant on other people, especially those living close to us with whom we have a greater connection.

I believe we weren't only created for a relationship with Jesus, but that this relationship is a very real relationship whilst we are still here on earth, waiting for either death or Jesus' return. I know my understanding of this relationship is still growing, but it's well worth the investment of time and effort.

My incident not only gave me time, but it also forced on me the need to be patient, as I just wasn't physically and mentally able to take on and do more.

My relationship with the Lord had always been quite sketchy and now, looking back, it's embarrassing to admit it and it seems so foolish. However, I knew the Lord could speak to us. He'd spoken to me to tell me to marry Sam. I'd heard the words in my head "She's the one for you." I'd acted on these words and it's the best thing I've ever done, so nothing and nobody could have convinced me that the Lord doesn't communicate with us, and I really believe it's His desire to communicate with us. However, He doesn't impose Himself on us. He allows us to come to Him, as children to a loving father. When we go to Him, He listens to us and communicates back to us. Just as a child with a father here on earth who might go and talk to Daddy, if the child then runs off to do something else, it doesn't hear what its father has to say back to it. I'd become very good at either not listening or not even staying around to see if my Father in heaven wanted to say anything to me.

My relationship with the Lord has been positively impacted by numerous things over the last seven years, many of which have been forced upon me by my circumstances. I'm going to share a few now, based on what has helped me most in my personal relationship with the Lord and what I'd loved to have known before (Would I have listened then? I'm not sure I would've, as I often liked to believe that I knew best. But also, I was impatient and wanted what I wanted, when I wanted it. The Lord doesn't work like this, and His patience is perfect. So either we fully commit to His timescale and way or we justify ourselves and what we get by other means).

What the brain/body injuries did for me, was stop me rushing around and forced me to create time to stop and wait, and in that stopping, in that waiting, I've been able to create the time and space to start to hear the Lord more clearly. The Lord certainly doesn't jump to our tune (to our whims), but He definitely wants a deep, personal relationship with each of us. The enemy definitely doesn't want us to have a deep, personal relationship with the Lord, so it's an area of spiritual warfare. What I've found is that by creating the space and having certain disciplines, the Lord has used this to teach me and lead me deeper into my relationship with Him. The disciplines that have worked for me, came about by "chance," in that many years ago I was given a book, by a much older mature Christian gentleman, that I'd often flicked through and picked up and put down, called "My Utmost for His Highest" (MUHH) by Oswald Chambers. I've now put it on the windowsill close to my bedroom and got into the habit of reading the daily devotional every day after lunch before I went up to bed. Through me getting into the habit of reading the devotional and then going to bed to sleep, I would get into bed and turn to the Lord in prayer as I lay down. Without thinking, I was making myself available to hear Him, not just rattling my prayers at Him or waiting expectantly for Him to answer me when I wanted Him to. I was just there, waiting, no expectation. What this created was an environment where the Lord was able to speak to me. This further helped through me keeping a notebook of my thoughts, so I could start to recognise His voice. The Lord started speaking to me in many different ways — but mainly through reading and other people.

MUHH's devotional on 6 December talked about the covenant relationship with God, that man has. We must step into that relationship with faith. God's done His bit; we do ours and then we have the choice as to whether we invest in developing the relationship. God will meet us and do as much as we want to develop the relationship, but our want needs to be based on actions, not just desires.

Marriage — wow, where do I start? It's the next relationship within my "tower," with only my relationship with the Lord being above it. It's a blessing that I believe goes far beyond what most of us can understand and articulate. If we're not careful, we settle for a marriage that is good, can appear great, when in reality it falls short of everything the Lord created marriage to be. We're living in a world where there are pressures on marriage from all sides (whether that's the general concept or right down to individual details in a single marriage), and whilst this is horrible, I not only don't think it's surprising, I think it's one of the best examples of how spiritual attack happens. We can get caught up in 'things' and try to play at being God, thinking we know better. Despite having all the best intentions, we are actually doing serious harm. I reiterate what I started by saying in this book: It's not for me to tell you how to live. You have that responsibility. However, I do believe that the Lord has allowed me to have a wakeup call, with a real shake up of what I believe is important. I now believe that life is all about relationships. After our relationship with the Lord, our marriage relationship is not only key to our happiness and wellbeing, but it's also key to the stability of our society. It shouldn't then be any wonder that it comes under so much attack. I believe that it's one of the foundations of the society we live in, whether we're Christians or not.

If you are a Christian, then hopefully you know that the Lord loves you personally and is your Father in heaven and the confidence and stability this gives you, in turn enables you to love your children as you're loved by the Lord. Growing up in a loving family, with a mother and a father, who both love each other and love their children, has to be the ideal situation. I know that we don't live in a perfect world — it is fallen and broken and whatever we do, it will remain this way until Jesus returns. But one thing we can do is celebrate and encourage people to get married and to take their wedding vows seriously. Most of us will know the vows, "For richer, for poorer," "In sickness and in health," "Until death do us part" and many of us will have publicly, probably in a church, said these same vows. But how many of us said them, really thinking that we'd be expected to knuckle down and live them out? Our personal desire is to focus on ourselves, however through marriage we stop being a single person; we become properly joined to another and through that union can be blessed with children. Those children will benefit hugely from the marriage of their parents not only surviving, but thriving and giving them the example of how life should be lived. My best mate Erik, suffered from going through a divorce, but he stayed close to our Lord throughout, and whilst it's not something you would wish on anyone, it's brilliant to see how the Lord has been able to turn it to good. Erik is now in a fabulous marriage with Jules, and alongside his 'day job' heads up "Divorce recovery" which is a course that's running all around the country, accompanied by a book, which helps people get back on their own two feet after all the challenges that a divorce brings. This is how our Lord can work, if we trust Him: He can bring great things out of apparent disasters. This doesn't make the situation any easier, but it's part of the hope we have; a hope that we can all have and a hope that should be a real driving force for all of us to help every marriage be the very best it can be.

The Lord then said to me that this tower needed to be supported by three guy ropes. As a very amateur sailor and also an unwilling camper, I was familiar with guy ropes, which are used to hold up a mast and with a quick look online I found that the word came from the Dutch in the early 1600s, who used it for the rope or wire that helps hold the mast up. They are installed radially, usually at equal angles around the structure they're holding up and really become effective and necessary when the structure comes under force, and would collapse. The Lord told me that my three guy ropes were to be a) health b) unpaid activities and c) paid activities. Preventing any of the three becoming over-tensioned and causing unnecessary stresses on the tower of relationships is becoming increasingly important, as my improvement continues.

This picture of the "tower," with the supporting "guy ropes," has been used many times over the last seven years, as you'll hear later in the book. Sometimes it's been necessary, embarrassingly, for the Lord to remind me of what He'd already told me to do, but again another example of His patience with us and His grace. He doesn't dictate, He allows us to choose how we live, but

He's been clear in telling us how He want us to live, loving our neighbour as we should love ourselves.

Once I'd made that step into recognising the importance of relationships and primarily my relationship with the Lord, the question I had, was "How do I develop this relationship?" I remember going to ask a number of people, who I knew or I thought had deeper, stronger and longer relationships with the Lord: I asked them how I should develop my relationship with Him. I was hoping for clear instructions and it really frustrated me when I felt they all fobbed me off, in different ways (it felt like being fobbed off without an answer). However, I was committed to developing this relationship and working out what the answer should be and I now believe that it will probably be the main thread running through all of the rest of my life, "How do I continue to develop the relationship I have with the Lord?"

In thinking about how to answer this and then do it, I looked at my other relationships and how I developed those which — given that my tower is all about relationships — it has been a good way to go. The short answer that I've found works for me, is "Time."

Whether it's the relationship with the Lord, my wife, the kids, friends etc., each relationship can only be developed by spending time with that person. The more time you spend with them, the more you get to know each other and the stronger the relationship becomes. The joy of building a relationship with the Lord is that He's always available to spend time with you. He doesn't need to put in a slot for you in His diary, which is brilliant, but in my experience this has actually made it harder to develop the relationship. If I want to get to know someone who is very busy and who has limited spare time, when I get a slot in the diary with them, I prioritise both making that appointment and using that time effectively. What I've found, was that I wasn't doing the same with the Lord, because I could always spend time with Him. It needed to suit me and it didn't become a priority. It was something I fitted around everything else I was doing. The busier I got, the easier it became to spend less time with the Lord and the downward cycle continues.

The challenge I put to you, is when someone asks you about prayer, or confesses to struggling to pray as they want to pray, please don't try and make them feel better by persuading them that it's the same for us all and that they're doing well. Compared to you and others, they may be doing better with their time in their relationship with the Lord, but I believe that it's one of the enemy's clever tactics to get us to settle for and even congratulate each other for a performance that's only good by comparison with what others are doing around us. Ultimately the relationship that other people have with the Lord and how they work on it is of no importance to our personal relationship with the Lord: that's between us and Him and it's up to us to do everything we can to make it as good as it can be. It's definitely worth the effort and that effort and time commitment will be different for everyone. What we need to do is work out how we can best encourage each other to keep working on that relationship, whether it's a new one for us or whether we've been in it for decades. Just as it is with people (even family members who we've known our whole lives), when we spend time with them — especially one-on-one — we learn more about them, about their experiences, their characters, their thoughts and desires.

So how have I developed my relationship with the Lord? I hesitated briefly about including this (as it will be different for each one of us), but I've included it, as I found it really frustrating to not be able to get anyone to give me what I thought was a clear answer. Simply realise that it's a question that you'll never fully answer until your dying day — even if you devote every moment you have to it, which isn't possible. What is fun though, is realising how deep and wide our Lord is and His whole being is Love. There's nothing about Him that isn't appealing (this is what I'm finding). The bits I might have been unsure about, or had a problem with, have all been down to my limited understanding.

"My Utmost for His Highest," Chamber's book, has a verse and a comment for every day of the year in order. What I found was that occasionally something from the verse or the text would jump out at me and set me thinking. Because I knew I was about to go to sleep and had a very poor short-term memory, I jotted down the thought so I could pick it up later. I had to do this in an ordered fashion, the same way each time, otherwise it wouldn't have worked for me. So, I put it in a notebook on my iPad and phone. This notebook automatically synchronised with my computer as well, so it was easy to access and always available. I have ended up putting the Kindle version of My Utmost for His Highest on my phone and iPad also, so that now I always have access to it, as and when I want it. This simple routine allowed me to focus on the Lord just before I went to sleep and as I laid down, I'd pray and ask Him to help and heal me. I'd ask Him to fill me with His Spirit and as He filled me, to flush away the toxins in my body and brain. One of the things I'd been told, was that I now had a greater susceptibility to dementia or Alzheimer's, due to the toxins in my brain from the injury. My prayer was that the Holy Spirit didn't just come and fill me, but as He filled me, He'd wash away everything that was bad. I'm not quite sure where all this thinking sits with what I'd call the "technical side of Christianity," but what I do know is that our Lord sent His Spirit to help us and I believe that repeatedly asking and therefore giving permission for the Spirit to fill me and cleanse me, has helped in my healing. Again, I reiterate that we have a very gracious God; He isn't going to force Himself on us, but He's waiting for us to turn to Him, to ask Him to give us what He longs to give us. His patience is way beyond our understanding. Sadly, at times we must be breaking His heart as we struggle "manfully" on, not asking for the help that He wants to offer. Imagine if one of your kids or family members was struggling, really needed help, but wouldn't ask for it and you couldn't give it until they asked.

As I continued to learn about developing my relationship with the Lord, I also wanted to develop my relationship with Sam and we started by getting into a morning routine of a cup of tea together in bed before we got up for the day. During this time we'd either read a daily devotional or use a bible app. We've currently settled on the YouVersion Bible app which has a verse and a short story for each day that's delivered by a video and then has a few pages with a devotional and a prayer. Again, it was about time, doing this repeatedly with Sam, getting into prayer together on a daily basis which developed both the relationship between us, and our relationship as a couple and individually with our Lord. We spend time together, sharing and communicating.

Developing my relationships in order, then leads me on to the relationship I have with my wife, Sam: Our marital relationship. The easiest thing to do now, would be to stop and say nothing, because whatever I write here, I risk offending or upsetting someone, which I have absolutely no wish to do. However, I haven't stopped here, because in my opinion, I believe that marriage, the union of a man and a woman, is a God ordained order created before the fall. At the start of the Bible, in the book of Genesis, we're told that Eve was made by God, from Adam's rib, to be his partner, his companion and helper, where the two working together would be much stronger and better than the one working alone. We don't have the privilege of living in the world as God created it to be, but we live in a fallen world with spiritual and physical battles being waged all around us, all the time. In this though, I believe that the more we can work together to have the world operating as God created it to be, the better it will be for all.

Strong marriages not only underpin society, but they're the bedrock on which so much that happens in our lives is built. The secure platform of a man and a woman, coming together in marriage, committed to each other, working together to support each other and to play to each other's strengths and cover for each other's weaknesses, is vital if we want the best global society we can have. Each of us gets to do our bit and collectively the difference we can make is huge. Supporting and championing marriage is the right thing and because it's the right thing for society, it's also one of the key areas for spiritual attack. In us believing that the Lord is real, it has to follow that the devil is also real and wants to destroy and tear down everything that is good and encouraging.

He wants to destroy as much as he can, while he's still allowed to roam the earth. The devil isn't an omnipresent force like the Lord — he needs to be selective in where he puts himself and what he does — and he'll put his resources to use where they can have most impact. I believe that one of these areas is marriage. If the devil can destroy marriage and weaken marriage, then he can go a long way to destroying the stability of humanity.

We're all continually taught that life is about what I want, what I need, and what I deserve. The problem with that is that it's all about us as individuals. One of the strongest institutions we have is marriage, where it's not about us personally, but about a couple: "I" becomes "We" and we work together for the good of each other. I don't think we should be surprised at the level of attack we have on marriage as an institution and also on individual marriages, with many ending in separation and divorce (often because one or both parties become focused on the "I"). We have similar challenges with our sexuality and I find it heart-breaking that we don't find it easier to discuss and get along with people that have very different opinions from ourselves.

I've said here where I stand, what I think, but that doesn't stop me wanting to relate and be friends with people that disagree with me. We all have the freedom of choice and different opinions are not only inevitable, but they're also good, as long as we can respect each other and disagree well and amicably.

I'll finish this little section with MUHH on 21 Jan, where it talks about "the kindness of thy youth" and the joy I'm now getting from wanting to and being able to invest in my marriage relationship, really hit me. I'd have found it all too easy to take Sam for granted: We've been married for thirty years this August and as I look at our marriage from a new perspective, I can see how the challenges of life, over the years, can easily allow an amicable partnership to become the status quo. I now believe that marriage is created to be far more than this. This new way of thinking, for me, comes from the renewing of my mind, which is not a passive occurrence, but a daily task. The time and effort to try and ensure my mind is renewed properly, is already well worth it and I'm certain will continue to be. Working on everything our marriage is capable of being and trying to understand what Sam really wants it to be like, is brilliant fun — a positive challenge with huge rewards.

Moving further down the relationship tree to work colleagues, we had a need in the business to get some help, which I cover in more detail in chapter twelve, "Paid activities." The reason for bringing it up now is that we, the business, engaged the services of a turnaround specialist called David Brands. He'd been selected through a process with the Cygnet senior management team and RSM (our advisors). He then came to see me for the final decision. He arrived at my office and within minutes informed me that I couldn't/wouldn't engage his services. I found this approach surprising and asked him why, to which he confidently told me that he knew about my strong Christian beliefs and because of these I would be unable or unwilling to work with him, as he was a committed atheist. I know this made me smile and my response was that this was fantastic. He looked shocked and I explained that he knew where I stood with my faith and he knew where he stood with his beliefs, about which he was happy to be open and clear; so, what was there to stop us working together? We had completely different opinions on a key matter, but we respected that each of us was free to our own opinion and we were happy to talk about it, if necessary. So we started working together, and I believe we worked very effectively. We recognised and acknowledged where we differed and had different opinions, but because it was all out in the open we were able to laugh at each other, as each of us thought the other was totally wrong, on a fundamental question. I loved it (not the fact that I thought David was wrong), but the fact that he had made a conscious decision about what he believed and therefore if the world was to end today, I would miss his company in heaven, but I wouldn't feel a responsibility for him, whereas, I'm of the opinion that so many of my mates, friends, acquaintances and people I've never met, have not made a conscious decision as to what they believe. What's going to happen to them? They've not consciously decided whether they believe that Jesus was God's son, born of a virgin on earth, who lived a spotless life and died on a cross, for all our sins, past present and future, so that we could be forgiven by our perfect, loving Father in heaven. Jesus conquered death when the Father raised Him after three days and we live in the promise that He will return.

I'm trying to use technology for the best and one of the things I like are the reminders on my iPhone popping up (which is great when your short-term memory struggles!). One of these is the verse in Luke's gospel (12:40), where it says, "You also must be ready, because the Son of Man will come at an hour when you do not expect Him." I'm not one to predict when this will be, but I'm confident it will happen and it could be in the next few hours after your reading of this, or another thousand years or so, but it will happen. When we face Christ, everyone will be in one of two camps, believers or non-believers, and then I believe it will be too late to change your mind. We all start in the non-believer camp and have to consciously believe, consciously accept, that Jesus is God's son and that by His death, our sins have been forgiven. If you look around you, maybe you yourself haven't consciously accepted who Jesus was and that His death was for you. If you haven't said "yes," and "thank you" to our Lord, you've automatically said "no." It's not about your actions, how well you think you live, how you compare yourself to everyone else, how well you think you're doing. It's all about Jesus and Him dying for you. I don't want any of my mates, friends, family, contacts, readers of this book, to be caught out, by not having made a conscious decision about what they personally believe. If any of them, or if you the reader, had an incident, like my cardiac arrest, and didn't survive, I don't want to be thinking "Why did I wait to say something? Why didn't I push them harder to make a decision?" So, I'm doing that now: Make your decision! Do whatever you need to do to get informed. Do it now. Don't wait. Your death is a certainty; it's the timing that's the unknown.

Again, I believe this is a key area of activity for the devil, it's much easier for him to put people off making a decision of any sort — him knowing that this is the same as them choosing no — than it is to persuade people who have committed their lives to Christ to change their minds. This battle is real and we're all on one side or the other of the yes/no line, at any point. The point of reckoning could, and will, come when we don't expect it. So, choose now and make a conscious decision what you believe and then move on with your life. I sincerely hope that you choose to believe as I do, but I respect whatever you decide — well done for making a decision! To everyone struggling to make a decision: Don't struggle! Do whatever you have to do in order to make your decision. Why? Because until you decide, you're in the "No" camp by default and I believe you'd only ever want to be there if you're absolutely, totally confident that Jesus wasn't the son of God, who died for your sins.

I continued to work on my physical health (I talk about exercise in chapter 10), but whilst exercising, I was listening to music and Sam asked me why I didn't listen to the Bible. I'd not thought about it and she said there was a great audio version read by David Suchet. That did it for me. So, I started listening to the Bible being read every time I exercised. Transformational.

The joy of relationships is that they're always changing, improving, worsening, but rarely if ever, staying the same. Today as I was pondering finishing this chapter, I felt the Lord say something along the lines of, "Hold on Matthew, here you're writing about the relationship you have with Me, but you're only writing about it from your perspective: how you want it to be, what you think it should be like and how excited you are about it. That's great, but have you ever thought about how I, your Lord, want the relationship to be like, what I want from it and what I feel about it?" It's been a humbling week for many reasons, but this was something else! Here I was approaching my relationship with the Lord and then making it all about me! Further on, in Chapter 9, I talk about how the Lord has been calling my attention to "pride" and yet here am I being so full of it; making the relationship I have with the Lord all about me.

I'll leave you with an extract from one of my daily devotionals, UCB's "Word for Today" (2 October 2022):

> *"In the 'Journal of Happiness Studies,' researchers looked at what distinguished quite happy people from less happy people. One factor consistently separated those two groups, and it's not about how much money you have; it's not about your health, security, attractiveness, IQ, or career success. What distinguishes consistently happy people from less happy people is the presence of rich, deep, joy-producing, life-changing, meaningful relationships. Social researcher Robert Putnam writes: 'The single most common finding from a half-century's research on life satisfaction, not only in the US but around the world, is that happiness is best predicted by the breadth and depth of one's social connections.' But you can know a lot of people without really being known by any of them and end up lonely. Those people in the New Testament Church got it right: it's in sharing with one another spiritually, emotionally, financially, and relationally that you achieve your highest level of joy."*

SECOND CHANCE

This perspective change to valuing relationships above everything, having an order to those relationships and then having them supported by the other areas of my life, has been phenomenal.

Chapter 6

P-perspective

"But you, man of God, flee from all this and pursue righteousness, godliness, faith, love, endurance and gentleness."

- 1 Timothy 6:11

"The Lord is my shepherd; I lack nothing. He makes me lie down in green pastures, He leads me beside quiet waters."

- Psalm 23:1-2

The Merriam-Webster dictionary describes "Perspective" as, "The capacity to view things in their true relations or relative importance."

Perspective is wonderful, but we humans can have very different perspectives on the same situation. I think this is fantastic and part of what makes us so powerful individually and even more powerful collectively. However, we need to learn to understand that our differences are there to be celebrated and enhanced by collectively working together, to play to each other's strengths and to support each other's weaknesses. This is one of those areas where there's no right or wrong — just differences.

Personally my wakeup call gave me, with the help of the Lord, a clear perspective on life and what I think is most important to me. This might be the same for others, but where it's been significant for me is that it's given me real clarity of what's most important and how parts of my life fit together. I'm now just trying to live, to put into practice what I feel has become clear to me.

The perspective (through the picture of the tower of relationships and the three guy ropes, each playing a supporting role especially in times where there's more external pressure) is so powerful, because I was often being led by the guy ropes getting over-tensioned and pulling my life out of balance, whilst I self-justified why I was doing what I was doing. A good example of this is how I exercised. I'd justified in my mind that going off cycling with a group on a Saturday morning was a good thing to do. It was keeping me healthy, it was a good example to my kids (when compared to the many negative things I could think of doing, such as going off to the pub, or lounging around drinking coffee and reading the paper after a big breakfast). What I'd missed and what insight was given to me by the picture of the tower was the perspective that the relationships in my life were the priority. Was me going off cycling in any way helping the family relationships? Was Sam happy about it?

There are many examples (see Chapter 10 for how I'd got cycling out of perspective) of how the guy ropes are only to support the integrity of the tower, the life of relationships — this has significantly affected my approach to life. Probably the biggest single change has been in the area of paid work (which I cover later in Chapter 12). It's on the one hand a very significant change, but it's also a very small change in that it's all about perspective and having a clear perspective on your life.

The perspective given by the tower, puts relationships at the heart of life and the key relationship is the one I have with the Lord. We covered that in the previous chapter, but the perspective of this relationship sitting at the top, consequently allows the rest of my relationships to be put in their rightful place. Rather than me jostling them around in my head — weighing up situations and making different calls — the perspective is unchanging; it's a clear picture of what's important and how it should be prioritised. I've found (and it's become increasingly so as I've recovered) that the ease with which I can find my mind developing reasons why I should do something that's not directly aligned with what I've been shown increases and increases, but every time I feel conflicted and step back, stop and look at the situation I'm dealing with from a distance, the perspective I want to have and the course I want to follow, is what the Lord has shown me.

Fear of the Lord: that's the only right and good kind of fear. Without fear, the temptation is to elevate our own sense of position and worth. Humility is vital for success in life. However, while I could have seen value in humility (or at least some humility), I saw it as a weakness to be overcome and I felt the need to make the most of what I thought I was capable of — of what I could do and of how I could help others. In later chapters, I'll touch on pride. My view of life revolved around me, what I could do, what I thought was right and how I could add value.

This perspective change to valuing relationships above everything, having an order to those relationships and then having them supported by the other areas of my life, has been phenomenal. These three guy ropes (health, paid and unpaid activities) attached to my tower are the other areas of my life, and seeing them as "only" guy ropes isn't all that transformational; however, it has been a real release. They're there to serve a purpose and sometimes that purpose is mission-critical to life. But even then, the purpose is to support the relationships. An easy example is paid work: For most of us, we know our relationships would really start to fall down if we didn't have any way of generating income to live, but so often we can get ourselves in a situation where instead of working to enable us to live our lives to the full, we end up being seduced into working more (for more money, with the promise that more money will buy us more life, more happiness). Money buys us nothing of true value and often gives us a more difficult lifestyle and even a reduced life expectancy. What a great way to have the devil rubbing his hands with glee at our stupidity! We could each have huge resources at our disposal, but we'll get nothing from these resources if we don't spend time using them for our own enjoyment and for the enjoyment of others.

SECOND CHANCE

I was struck by how I'd always been able to do most things, but because I'd seen them as so normal, I hadn't appreciated them. It was only by being forced to stop and think, that I truly gained the necessary appreciation for them.

Chapter 7

A-appreciation

"Finally, brothers and sisters, whatever is true, whatever is noble, whatever is right, whatever is pure, whatever is lovely, whatever is admirable — if anything is excellent or praiseworthy — think about such things. Whatever you have learned or received or heard from me, or seen in me; put it into practice. And the God of peace will be with you."

- Philippians 4:8-9

I call this "morning tea!" It's something so simple, yet it still strikes me strongly every day and I hope it continues to do so.

I've always been a morning person and am generally happy to wake up and get on with the day. However, what I've realised is that my view of myself in the mornings, was when I was comparing myself to other people and their response to mornings. Comparison is one of the big influencers of how we appreciate things (or think we are appreciating things). I've had a very simple and basic life lesson, with what I've been through, regarding appreciation and how I wasn't appreciating most of the basics in my life — and I mean really appreciating them!

I was fortunate to go through the reality of suddenly not being able to do many basic things and so when I could do something again, my appreciation of being able to do it was huge. As I thought more about these things, I was struck by how I'd always been able to do most things, but because I'd seen them as so normal, I hadn't appreciated them. It was only by being forced to stop and think, that I truly gained the necessary appreciation for them.

What I'm about to describe is potentially something that you, the reader, do virtually every morning, or at least some mornings:

It starts with waking up and being aware that you've woken up. Then comes the ability to get out of bed, swing your legs around, put your feet on the floor and stand up. Then putting one foot in front of the other, you'd walk to the door and out of the bedroom. I then have the stairs to navigate as I go to the kitchen (I live in a house with stairs!). I walk down the stairs and can do this by putting one foot after the other on alternate stairs. Just writing it seems a bit silly, but I'd always taken it for granted that I could walk downstairs this way and it was only losing the ability to do it, needing to hold on to the bannister rail for quite some time, that I was made/enabled to really appreciate the ability to walk downstairs, without holding on. I'd certainly always taken this for granted and it was only once losing the ability to do this and then needing to hold on to the banister rail for quite a few weeks, that it made me really appreciative of the ability to walk downstairs without holding on.

I then would walk into the kitchen, where I'd be able to get fresh water out of a tap and fill a kettle, which I'd then plug in and flick a switch on to get the water to boil. 'Wow! Fresh running water and electricity in my house. I'd open a cupboard, take out two mugs, take out two tea bags, put them in the mugs, pour the boiling water and make tea. Whilst the tea would be brewing, I'd go and take my morning pills and then I'd add fresh milk that's kept cool behind another door in something called "a fridge." This is where it excited me: that I could then proceed to pick up two full mugs of tea (one in each hand) and carry them up the stairs, without spilling them, into my bedroom. I can vividly remember not being able to do this when I was first out of hospital. I'd then walk through the door into my bedroom and there asleep in my bed would be a beautiful woman (the love of my life and woman of my dreams), whom I could wake up with a kiss as I'd put her cup of tea down on her bedside table.

I'd then be able to pull the curtains back the looking out over our front garden, the road that passes our house and the field opposite — where normally a couple of horses would be waiting for their breakfast. I'd then be able to climb back into bed, pick my cup of tea up and have some time with the Lord and Sam before anything else starts. I'd go through this routine daily and it'd start me off so well. I've made this an enjoyable habit that I stick to everyday I possibly can.

I find that it's very easy to become negative even when the blessings are huge and we live in a world where negative news appears to make much stronger headlines. However, this in turn means that we're surrounding ourselves with a negative approach; constantly looking at what's not right, what could be better, what needs changing. There's definitely a place for making things better and not accepting second best (improvements), because without this we'd also just regress as a society. But we do need to learn to improve and to change with a positive mindset.

It really hit me when I was exercising on my Concept2 rowing machine and I signed myself up for one of their challenges: It was called the "April Fool's challenge" and it meant rowing 1000m on the first day of April and increasing this by 1000m each day, until I had to row 30,000m on the 30 April. It quickly became a chore and a negative part to my life, starting to have an impact on other parts of my life and the people around me. I needed a conscious reset one morning, to focus on the amazing privilege I had to physically be able to take on this challenge, to have access to a rowing machine every day, to have the time in the day to do it. All these blessings were there and here I was getting negative about something that I should have been appreciating.

I was reading Selwyn Hughes' book "The Laws of Spiritual Success," where on page fifty-one he talks about Psalm 103 being all about choosing to praise God. A law of personality is that what we choose to think about, will soon affect the way we feel. This is so true! But we need to consciously choose what we think about and how we go about this. We all have a Father in heaven, who knows us and loves us. Do we appreciate this? Most of us have (or will have had), parents that love us. Do we appreciate them and if we're parents do we appreciate the gift of children? I reckon that a number of you reading this, will have thought "yes" and then immediately followed that thought with a "but" of some kind. I'd call that human nature, but it's very easy to get into ruts in our life where we don't fully appreciate what we have, or what's going on around us. We also don't encourage others to fully appreciate what they have in their lives. We often find it easier to take a negative view of something and to try and empathise with someone else having a negative experience, rather than being comfortable fully appreciating our blessings. If we see our children really enjoying and appreciating an experience, or a toy, it gives us joy and I'm sure it gives our Father in heaven joy when we appreciate what we have. Could most situations be better? Yes, of course they could, but that shouldn't prevent us from fully appreciating what we have and encouraging those around us to do the same. I've found that putting things around me (such as pictures and notes) and having reminders pop up on my phone, really help, as they stop me from going down the wrong tracks during the day. Being able to appreciate something or see the good in something, even when there's stuff that's not ideal, is a wonderful way to align your demeanour with good decision-making for the future.

We are commanded to be thankful. It's easy to not appreciate something until we don't have it. The thing that springs to mind is power: It's not until we have a power cut — until our continual supply is interrupted — that we realise what a blessing it is. The Bible instructs us to be thankful.

Continue committing to Jesus. Always have deep gratitude. Nothing can impact this, however hard or difficult life may seem.

Why do I find it so difficult to accept — simply accept — that God is real?

Chapter 8

R-real

"That is why we labour and strive, because we have put our hope in the living God, who is the Saviour of all people, and especially of those who believe."

- 1 Timothy 4:10

This is where the story starts to get interesting: It's certainly where I'd say my life started to change in a measurable way. I knew I was a Christian, I knew I'd done an Alpha course in the early nineties and Emma had forced me to stop "pratting around" and make a decision — Jesus was either real or He wasn't. I'd experienced various events in the next twenty-three years where things had happened that the Lord had been instrumental in, and I'd willingly admit to being a firm believer in Christ and His teaching. I used to pray and would primarily justify myself with the thought that God had given me certain gifts and I needed to use those gifts in the way I felt was best. It was an interesting and I'd guess fairly normal and common "Christian" lifestyle.

Now I needed help. I didn't have the words to articulate what I was feeling and all I knew was that I needed God to help me. I was at the end of my tether; life was beyond me being able to manage, let alone control what was happening. So I turned to the Lord and asked for help. I was beyond being able to help myself, beyond seeing the solution that I wanted and beyond asking the Lord for anything but help. And so He helped me. His grace is truly amazing and those moments I'll carry with me to my dying day (which I'm looking forward to — but more of that later!).   There I was, asking for help, nothing more and the Lord held me. It was just like when I, as a father, had one of my little children in need of reassurance: I'd pick them up and hold them with my arms wrapped around them. The Lord did this to me. I felt His embrace around me — His lovingly firm and secure embrace. I clearly felt His fingers gripping my upper arms as He held me. It was the embrace of an adult to a child; safe, secure, firm and loving. Nothing more and nothing less. It enabled me to slip straight into sleep; not worrying about anything. This happened four or five times over about a ten-day period and it will live with me, to my dying day, as probably the most significant experiences of my life.

At the time, it didn't feel like anything really significant (which is as odd to write as it probably is to read), but it was just something comforting and necessary. However, the impact of knowing that God is real and not just a good bet (not highly likely, but really real — 100% real), has a knock-on effect of huge magnitude. This is where we are all different and different in so many ways and that's part of God's design. But I can't encourage you strongly enough to accept that God is real — really real. Even if there's a nagging doubt (whether it's a huge doubt or a tiny 1% grain of doubt), put it out of your mind and live as if God is real. Make it a priority to never let that grain of doubt get a foothold or dwell in your mind, because we're in a battle! A real battle! I wouldn't want to over-spiritualise this, but it's as important to not underplay it.

When the Lord becomes real; when the Father, God, the Son, Jesus and the Holy Spirit become real, then so does Satan, the devil and the Word of God. We're told in

Scripture about Satan: we're told to watch out for him and that he prowls around, looking to deceive and destroy. He's already beaten, but until Jesus comes again, which He will, we need to remember that God's real and His word is His promise to us. We're told to be vigilant and the last thing the enemy, the devil, wants is for any of us to truly believe in Jesus. In my experience over the last six years, the spiritual attack is very subtle and it's not the enemy coming at me in any overt way, like a bulldozer destroying a house. No, it's the very subtle chipping away at small parts of the structure that are integral to its rigidity and robustness. The last thing the enemy wants is for us to fully put our trust in Jesus.

This might seem fearful and some of you reading this might be tempted to think that you don't want to antagonise an enemy who might fight back, but that's just what the devil wants! However, Jesus has already won this battle and standing in His name, which we're called to do, is all about claiming the victory and the enemy will flee. So there's nothing to fear, there's only a victory that was won on our behalf to claim. But we can't claim that victory until we truly believe that Jesus Christ is real, that Jesus died on that cross to defeat death and our enemy and that He did that for us. For nearly twenty-five years I'd known this in my head, but I hadn't known it in my heart. I hadn't been willing to fully accept what I believed and I'd allow nagging doubts to put down little roots and stop my head from being totally committed. The wonderful news though, is that living life knowing Jesus is real. Knowing that we have a loving Father in heaven and knowing that He knows everything about us (down to the very hairs on our head; or not, for some of us!), means we don't need to worry about anything.

In May 2021 I was on a course with the NorthWest Gospel Partnership (NWGP) and I was asked to pray. Despite being a Christian since the early nineties, this was the first time that I really felt I was talking to and being heard by, the living God. Prayer is very significant! It's a huge blessing, privilege and opportunity to be able to turn to God and for Him to hear us. How should we use prayer properly? He hears and He's real!

Why do I find it so difficult to accept — simply accept — that God is real? Even now I catch myself questioning and wondering whether perhaps, if I hadn't had such a strong physical encounter with the Lord to confirm His presence and wipe away my doubts, I'd still be in a place of questioning, doubting and rationalising God and that this path is of no use to anyone. God wants us to believe in Him, to trust Him, to let go of what we may have been taught or what we may have taken on. Then and only then will God walk with us. In the next chapter, I try and explain how the Lord dealt, (unfortunately I should probably say "is dealing") with my pride. That's the obstacle that I needed to overcome and continually need to keep overcoming. The more I wrestle with why I struggle accepting that God is real, the more I'm reaching the conclusion that a "real" God is far more terrifying, awe-inspiring and awesome than I'm naturally willing to deal with. We're told in the Bible that He sees us and that He knows us and whilst this is wonderful, I find it terrifying and I'm sure others do to (if you're being honest with yourself). Everyone knows what parts of their life, whether thoughts or actions, they don't want others to see. To accept that God knows us, sees us and that He's a real present God, is hard to cope with. It should be hard, but it should also be wonderful and life changing.

Union with Christ is a real thing — it's not just something other people talk about. If I was in a group of people, especially people I respected, I wouldn't question things that they seemed to take for granted. I'd probably try and keep quiet and stay on the edge of the conversation. Union with Christ was one of those topics. There's a book titled, "Union with Christ" written by Tim Keller, that I thoroughly recommend. I could throw my tuppence in about Bible study, prayer, being filled with the Spirit etc., but being honest, regarding union with Christ, I didn't understand what I was talking about. I didn't know what questions to ask, so I just rambled along satisfying myself that I thought I was doing comparatively well. The comparison trap again — it's irrelevant! What I was missing and potentially could've missed forever, was that the Lord wants a real, hour by hour, minute by minute, relationship with each one of us. However, it doesn't just happen. I find this example really useful (probably because I'm a big bloke that can't dance and in my pre-marital days, it was much more common for the guy to ask a girl to dance):

So, picture this — you see the most beautiful girl you've ever seen from across the room; alone. Do you ask her to dance? Assuming no alcohol is involved, the answer is probably no. I'd be thinking, if she says yes, then what? I'd just embarrass myself, potentially publicly and be left hanging; when she walks off back to her mates laughing (and that's assuming she said yes). I think for many people it feels to them like this with Christ and entering into a relationship with Him. The reality though is so different and the difference is miraculous. In Christian terms, it's "grace" and a miracle, but you have to ask the girl to dance with you. Even though you've been told she'll say "yes," you have to believe it. It's so easy to see yourself as you think she sees you; as you think you'd see yourself. NO, NO, NO! It's just not like that — we can all, every single one of us, know that if we ask Christ to dance, then the answer will be yes and as the greatest dancer ever, He will lead at the right pace and in the right way. He definitely won't let us lead and try and tell Him how to dance. We know it would be stupid trying to tell the best dancer how to dance with us and it's equally silly when we try and tell the Lord how to work with us; in union with us.

"I have been crucified with Christ and I no longer live, but Christ lives in me. The life I now live in the body, I live by faith in the Son of God, who loved me and gave Himself for me." - Galatians 2:20

"God told Joshua, 'Stretch out the spear that is in your hand toward Ai, for I will give it into your hand'" (Joshua 8:18 NKJV).

It's amazing how courageous you feel when God is backing you up. When you know He is on your side, you can say, "No weapon formed against me will prevail" (see Isaiah 54:17). But overconfidence is self-confidence that's not based on God-confidence. Our problem is, we plan, say, and do things without first checking to find out if God is behind us. Do you remember what the evil spirit said to those trying to mimic Paul's ministry when they weren't empowered by God's Spirit?

"Jesus I know, and Paul I know; but who are you?" (Acts 19:15 NKJV)

When you're under spiritual attack, you need to know that:

1. You're in right standing with God (2 Corinthians 5:19);

2. It's God's fight as well as yours (see 2 Chronicles 20:15) and

3. "Whatever you bind on earth will be bound in heaven, and whatever you loosen on earth will be loosed in heaven" (Matthew 18:18 NIV).

There must be agreement in both realms. If it's not approved where God is, it shouldn't be approved where you are. Your confidence comes from knowing you're operating in His will. The Bible calls us "labourers together with God" (1 Corinthians 3:9 KJV), so you can't go off and do your own thing. Don't try moving any mountain the Lord doesn't want moved, or raising anybody from the dead except the Lazarus He calls forth. We do on earth only what He has declared to be His will in heaven. And He backs us up!

Think how inspiring it would be if we each encouraged one another to make the most of what we've each been given and celebrated each other's successes in this area.

Chapter 9

Guy Ropes & Further Advice (lmNOp)

"For everything in the world — the lust of the flesh, the lust of the eyes, and the pride of life — comes not from the Father but from the world."

- 1 John 2:16

Earlier in chapter 5, when I introduced my Tower of relationships, I touched on the guy-ropes that are there to support the tower. These guy ropes are the things that we do in life to support our relationships.

Some of you might already know, but in my simple picture a guy rope is something that's attached to an upright structure in order to stabilise it and protect it from falling over. These are especially useful when there's stress that can potentially destabilise and knock over the structure. My personal experience with guy ropes has been with tents but I also see them as the shrouds attached to the mast of a boat. They're in position to provide the maximum strength and help with the minimum interference in the operation of the primary structure.

So, our lives, our tower, the "tower" of relationships, is supported by these three guy ropes — especially when things go wrong. These three guy ropes need to be as strong, but also as small and unobtrusive as possible. I found that I'd started, even gone a long way, to making the guy ropes as important, potentially even more important, than the tower in my life. The tower and the perspective of it, with the guy ropes, has mainly been covered in chapter 5. Moreso, what I found was that knowing it was one thing, but living it was something completely different. Whether this is a bit of spiritual warfare, or just my innate stupidity, I'll probably never know. However, I struggle, progressively more and more, with living and prioritising my tower of relationships and keeping my three guy ropes of health, paid and unpaid activities, appropriately tensioned and positioned in my life. In practice, I found that I was making compromises and trade-offs; debates that started in my mind but ended up being acted out in practice.

It wasn't as easy as it sounds, but in essence I turned to the Lord and asked for help. The great thing I've found about my burgeoning relationship with Him, is that He appears to accept my stupidity and silliness and is just as willing to help me over something I know I should be able to do now, as He is to help me with something really difficult and challenging. A great lesson for us all, is knowing that our Creator God wants to work with us, wherever we are and with whatever we're dealing with. All we have to do is engage with Him and invite Him in to help. So here I was struggling and eventually I turned to the Lord and asked for help. It wasn't an instantaneous response, but I got a response and it was a strong feeling of being told, with a smile, that He recognised that I wasn't that bright and that He needed to keep it simple for me. I fully expect that when we get to heaven, we're going to find that our Lord has a great sense of humour and there's going to be a lot of fun and laughter. Any way, He told me that He thought I'd probably got my alphabet nailed, so in keeping it simple, all I had to remember was a short part of it, and that part was "l, m, n, o, p." He then asked me what word I could see, whereupon I, being a little slow, struggled to respond. So He gave me the hint that it was two letters and the "NO" popped out. The Lord then said that the "no" related to the letters "l," "m" and "p." The "l" for Lust, the "m" for Materialism and the "p" for Pride. Wow — you can imagine how that hit me! So much so, that I simply went to sleep!

Whilst living life to PAR is the main bit, the practicalities of living out "l,m,NO,p" daily, has been the awakening for me. I'll deal with each of them individually below, but I fear I'm only just scratching the surface and that my remaining years on earth will be spent moving forward with the reality of how to live life properly: saying "no" to the "l, the "m" and the "p." I'm sure that every single one of us struggles with temptation in some way and I think part of the problem is that because we struggle, it's easier to sympathise with other strugglers and potentially normalise the temptation, rather than fight against it. I've generally found that when I've turned to friends for help, their desire to help has been strong and their motives have been good, but the actual help received has been short of what I needed, and mainly because of a willingness they had to want to try and make me feel they understood me, by sharing their similar struggles. This definitely has its place and benefits, but in my experience what I need are friends who will walk with me, alongside me, through the struggles, but never normalise the battle. I think "battle" is a good word, because I've found that in areas of my life where I've succumbed to temptation, the desire to fall a bit further, and then a bit further, over time, just continues. If we're tempted, we need to flee from it completely and then do everything possible to never let ourselves get pulled back. Good examples of this are drugs, alcohol or pornography: all have the ability to completely destroy lives and anyone that finds they're tempted by them must flee from them. The great thing is we're all different, but the challenge that this throws up is that some of us can manage things with no problems and others struggle at the slightest hint. One of the people in my life that had the biggest impact was my uncle: he struggled with alcohol as a young man when he started work in London and decided he had to give it up. With the help of AA, he successfully never touched another drop for the rest of his life. I really enjoy a drink, but I'm fairly certain alcohol isn't a temptation that is strong for me. However, the temptation of pornography has an appeal that I know I have to resist because I could allow myself to be led down the wrong path.

Lust - I strongly debated mentioning in this book that I've had to actively deal with the temptation to pornography, because it's not something I find easy to admit and it would've been simpler to just not mention it. However, to not mention it would've been wrong for two reasons: Firstly, it could've been a first step for me to justify hiding something that I'm not proud of, and in hiding it, even slightly, it's a small step in the wrong direction. It's these tiny, often semi-justifiable actions that we need to fiercely resist. The battle with pornography has been an important fact over the last seven years, because the Lord has shown me that there's a better way of living and it's not possible to live really well and have really fruitful lives, if we succumb to temptations. The second reason is that if only one person who reads this is struggling with a pornography addiction and it helps them, then it's worth it. We're in a spiritual battle and the enemy knows where we're weak. He's cunning and devious and will attack each and every one of us at our weakest point. So, I mention this because someone reading this will be struggling with pornography or drugs or alcohol or gambling, etc. You don't need to go on struggling, but you do need to choose the direction you want to go. Take the first step down the right path and gather around you friends and acquaintances who will support and help you every step of the way. If any of them, ever, allow you to justify your poor behaviour, strongly question who is in your inner circle of "friends" regarding the matter that you're battling. You can make it easier for yourself by dealing with it in the Lord's power, rather than struggling along by yourself. However, to tap into this, you've first got to decide whether you're really willing to believe that He's real.

We weren't made to live lives that are a constant battle with temptation and so me saying "no" to my "l," "m" and "p" has not only been freeing, but it's also taken me to a whole new level of satisfaction in life. I could easily fall into lust, materialism or pride, any day, but I believe that being aware of that, being open about it, keeping it up in the light, not only makes it easier to deal with, but it ensures that it isn't allowed to grow in the dark until it becomes unmanageable. The strongest weapon the enemy has here, is keeping what's tempting us and leading us astray in the dark. If we can feel ashamed about what we're doing and try to hide it, then the likelihood of us struggling more is increased, as is the likelihood of others struggling more with the same thing. We're called to do life together and this is to share our successes and our struggles. I hope and pray that in being open about my struggle with pornography, will enable other people to not only talk about their struggles, but to deal with them fully. We can all be free of whatever temptation is pulling us down, but we all have to want that freedom for ourselves and others and then work together to achieve it. In the Lord's eyes, no sin like we're discussing here is greater than another: He loathes all of them and He wants us free. You might struggle with this, because we humans get comfort from ranking sin on a scale and then using it to justify ourselves. I'm not going to go into detail here about how the Lord wants to set us free, apart from saying that the Holy Spirit, a part of the Trinity with the Father and the Son, is a gift from God that wants to work with us and help us. If you're struggling with some form of temptation, any form and at any depth, you can be totally set free.

Materialism - Philippians 4:12-13 says, "I know what it is to be in need and I know what it is to have plenty. I have learned the secret of being content in any and every situation, whether well fed or hungry, whether living in plenty or in want. I can do all this through Him who gives me strength" (NIV).

Ecclesiastes 4:6 says, "It is better to have only a little, with peace of mind than be busy all the time with both hands, trying to catch the wind" (GNT).

Both of these verses have always sat relatively comfortably with me, however when I look back on my life now, I had it so confused and messed up. I'd fallen for the worldly view of provision and the benefits from that provision. I believe that it's good to want nice things and to want to achieve things and enjoy whatever you've got. But when the acquiring becomes a way of life, just for the sake of the acquisition and comfort and when the apparent safety comes from the accumulated wealth and goods — then it's bad. Before I had my wake-up call, I was working really hard to grow the business. In my mind to provide for my family, and to enable us to do great things with both the business and with the family. Whilst these things are lovely, was the desire to accumulate and the sacrifice that the desire demanded, worth the benefits that were won? I'm not sure they were and I'd like to have spent more of my time investing directly into the relationships in my life and a little less in what I could do for those around me.

We as a country are wealthy and virtually all of us have the opportunity to live great, healthy lives, but we often fall for the push from the world of "you deserve more," "look what they've got" and "you should have that." This is a temptation that needs to be killed off, just like the earlier temptations we talked about. But it's become so pervasive in our culture that it's now celebrated. I think you'll find that we're more interested in and lift up people, that have more, as opposed to celebrating and lifting up people that have "made the most" of what they've been given. Think how inspiring it would be if we each encouraged one another to make the most of what we've each been given and celebrated each other's successes in this area; with the total amount accumulated being merely a measure of how well or not someone is doing at making the most of what they're responsible for.

I feel that my Lord is going to hold me accountable for what I've done with my life, the opportunities I've had, the gifts I've been given and I want to hear Him say "Well done good and faithful servant," when I meet Him in heaven (see Matthew 25). I'm certain He's not going to congratulate me on what I've been able to buy, the holidays I go on or the house I lived in. But I think He'll hold me accountable for how I've used what He's given me and the positive difference I've been able to make in the part of the world that I'm connected to.

Pride - For me this has been the big one and as I continue to improve, it will be again, if I let it. I like things my way. I think I know best and I want people to do what I want. It's useful that this word is spelt the way it is: the middle letter says it all. I now write it pr"I"de, as it's the "I" that I need to be aware of. Looking back over my life, much of my success came because of what "I" was able to achieve. It was fairly easy for me to believe that I knew what I was doing — certainly better than most people — and that the way forward was to just get people to follow what I was doing, where I wanted to go and how I wanted to do it. If I hadn't been pulled out of life so completely, this would've carried on in some form or other. But I believe as I look back, everyone would've been the worse for it. Self-confidence is good, but so is humility and it's really important to understand how small and insignificant each and every one of us is. We have a Father in heaven, who made the earth and provided everything in the earth for us to live as we now live. He also provided this galaxy and other galaxies, and He created all this by speaking. I certainly can't properly get my head around the enormity of God and then the reality, that He knows and wants to know me personally, individually. He wants to indwell me with His Holy Spirit and cares about my day-to-day needs. In this reality, how can I be so full of myself and what I want, when and how I want it, when I'm so insignificant? When I see an ant run across the floor, it makes me think not only how big the gulf is between me and the ant, but that the gulf between me and God is probably even bigger, and that's despite us being created in His image. Pr'I'de is the main thing that I'm trying to tame, so that I learn how to live appropriately, as God created me to live, without it being about the "I." Galatians 2:20 sums up where I'm at now: "I have been crucified with Christ and I no longer live, but Christ lives in me. The life I now live in the body, I live by faith in the Son of God, who loved me and gave Himself for me."

Chapter 10
Guy Rope 1 –
Health, Mental & Physical

"Do you not know that your bodies are temples of the Holy Spirit, who is in you, whom you have received from God? You are not your own."

- 1 Corinthians 6:19

I think this is an area that affects and impacts everyone in really different ways. I think that everyone would agree that having good mental and physical health is a positive thing — something that we'd all have in an ideal world. The thing is though that we don't live in an ideal world. This is when the questions start as to why some of us don't have the health we'd like. A lot of these reasons have some validity, but for me it comes down to responsibility and that is firstly "how responsible am I at looking after my own mental and physical well-being?" And secondly "how well am I at helping others to look after theirs?"

We live in a society where most of us say we want to take responsibility for things, but it's also a society where we find it hard to accept responsibility when things don't go as well as we think they should. So, if we're not as healthy as we think we should be, it's much easier to accept if the fault lies outside our control; ideally with someone or something else. However, we're the ones that suffer if we let our mental or physical sides be anything less than "as good as possible." I'm a great example of this: I could blame my cardiac arrest and the subsequent situation I found myself in on my genetic makeup or on having to work too hard. I was, after all, exercising and trying to keep fit. Or was I? Perhaps I was using exercise as an escape from normal life; an area where I could ostensibly keep nearly full control over and enjoy only having myself to worry about. It was probably the latter, but it didn't need to be.

It really hit home for me about 2 years into my recovery, when my young son, who was eight at the time, announced over breakfast one Saturday morning how much he liked having me there at breakfast. I thought he meant that he was pleased I'd survived and could be with them, so I happily agreed that I was also glad I'd survived and was with them. But then he replied, "No Dad, it's nice that you're not out cycling!" As the saying goes, "Out of the mouths of babes..." That really did hit me hard! Here was an eight-year-old, my eight-year-old, telling me that he'd missed not having me around on a Saturday morning because I was out cycling. I'm pretty certain that whilst I loved being out cycling with the Frodsham Wheelers, I also thought that I was being a great dad — I was being a good role model of a father and working hard to provide for my family, exercising to stay healthy, not going off drinking and indulging in other unhealthy and costly pursuits. However, at the end of the day all my son was seeing was an absent father that he wanted to spend time with. I don't think he wanted anything special. He just wanted my time, my presence and us all being together. There will be some people, men and women, who might be tempted to use this paragraph as a weapon to try and persuade a partner or family member to change what they do, because they think it would be better. After all is said and done, that choice can only be made by the individual concerned. Be really careful with anything you do or say and ensure it leads to the result you're looking for! I truly hope that that includes improved, long term relationships for everyone involved.

I agree with my son now: I do think there's a right balance to be struck. I also think it's a balance that we find hard to strike alone. Sam, my wife, wants me to be healthy and is happy for me to go off cycling, as she knows that it's good for me. However, she also doesn't understand as she hasn't personally experienced the pleasure that I get from exercising. This is a guy rope where I find it really easy to get the tensioning and positioning wrong and as I return to living a full life, it's really important that I get this balance right. I'm doing this with a combination of accountability and sensible goals. I'm now looking at my life from the perspective of managing my wellbeing for every day that the Lord gives me, whether that's another fifty or another five years. If it's going to be fifty, I need to sensibly manage my health in order to allow me to be the best sixty-, seventy-, eighty-and/or ninety year old Matthew. This means managing my weight, my flexibility, my strength, my heart (blood pressure and pulse) and my brain. This is how I look at it. I have no medical training, but I'm learning what works best for me. For the above basic list, I generally manage it in the following way:

Weight - I want this to be a combination of kilograms and body fat, which I measure every Monday morning and my scales record it. I find that recording it really helps to keep me honest with myself. While I struggle to be where I want to be, I don't think my approach to being healthy is being anything but positive on the family. I still enjoy a drink; just not every night and then only with Sam or friends. We try and eat a healthy diet and enjoy our food and mealtimes together as a family as much as we possibly can.

Flexibility - This has been a bigger issue and I've suffered with lower back issues since I was a teenager and am well acquainted with my local chiropractor. Now, however, I'm keen to deal with my back issues properly, once and for all, rather than just to get it good enough so that I can keep going for the next period of however many months. I want a robust back that will last me to one hundred and I'm sensing that this is possible, if I'm willing to do the work. I've started being serious about Pilates and am amazed at what my body has nearly lost the ability to do; the muscles that I've either not developed or not trained to perform as they were designed. It's going to be a very slow process, but I'm finding that I'm starting from a very low point, so progress is reasonable and the prize is fantastic. The challenge is having trained myself for over forty years to just manage and carry on. Understanding how many "old" people get into long term life difficulties as a result of a fall, should be a huge wake up call to us all to deal with our stability and balance while we still can. At some of my Pilates classes there are men and women well into their seventies, some in their eighties, who are improving monthly, just by doing the classes and not giving up. I find them inspirational.

Strength - This is something I think we all take for granted — I certainly did! Whether we're comparatively strong or not, we know that we'll lose it as we age. However, it's so easy to not do anything about it and justify to ourselves that we're doing okay through comparing ourselves with others. I don't want that. That's why I started doing something simple with my thirteen-year-old son: press-ups every morning,. I'm fascinated at how this can become routine and relatively easy after a few months and other exercises can be added that bolster strength using body weight, all taking minimal time. Proper weights need to start soon.

Heart - We've all got one and we need to look after it. I now monitor my pulse and take my blood pressure every three days. Again, it's easy to pick up on trends and vary exercise and other activities if it's not looking right, which in turn appears to allow my body to deal with common ailments, such as a cold, much more effectively.

I wasn't aware of the impact my high cholesterol level could be having on my system. I hadn't correlated that number with the potential build-up of deposit in my arteries proving a health risk. It's as stupid as it sounds, but I just hadn't made the link. I thought I was healthy. I'd always been relatively healthy. I'd never smoked, done drugs or drunk alcohol excessively and I exercised on a regular basis. When I looked around, there were many people in a far worse position or so I arrogantly thought and left it at that. I now realise how easy it is to measure things like pulse and blood pressure at home, which with an annual check-up by the GP, keeps everything at bay and ultimately isn't only helping you, but by being healthy, it's helping not put any strain on a creaking National Health Service. We can so easily bitch and moan about our Health Service and some of it's justified, but how much more should each of us be doing to ensure that we don't become a burden of any sort!

Strengthening my heart became the reason why I returned to exercise, and I was told by my cardiologist that during my incident, when my heart was stopped, parts of it would have died and these bits won't recover. However, the rest of the heart will adapt and slowly compensate for the bits that aren't working. As a layman, I've been fascinated with the basic information I've picked up about how our hearts work and how clever they are. I was measured and given a maximum heart rate I could work up to and told, in no uncertain terms, that this was never to be breached. I was then informed that I needed to manage my "area under the line" — the line being my heart rate, measured on the y-axis of a graph, with time along the x-axis. If I was going to be exercising for longer, then the line needed to be lower to control the area. It was a fairly simple instruction and one I've found relatively easy to follow, but I've been careful to not cycle or exercise in situations where I could get competitive and do something stupid — especially as I feel so fit.

Brain - I'm delighted mine is still working and it's been eye opening to have it not functioning and then slowly and steadily start to return to the level of performance I'd expect. Probably most startling from the brain injury, is that when I can't do something mentally, I'm generally not aware that I can't do it until the point when I can do it and I then realise what I couldn't do and then all sorts of situations fit into place. It's been most noticeable around the area of data manipulation and my colleagues at work must have found it phenomenally frustrating, because I could look at data for a board meeting and agree a course of action and then a few months later I'd be looking at the same data and would see another course of action that I thought was better. Then, I'd quite simply want to pursue it even though I'd previously agreed with them what we'd do. I just found it exciting that I could, in my opinion, analyse data better and see a better way forward. So, I assumed that everyone would immediately agree with me and want to do what I now thought was best. Life's not like that and the 'I' was rearing its ugly head.

Getting my brain back to full health and functioning fully, is probably going to take another few years and then it's a lifelong exercise to keep it well. I was told early on in rehab, that the cardiac arrest and the fall from the bike, would both probably cause toxins to be created in my brain and that these toxins would increase my likelihood of getting a condition such as Dementia or Alzheimer's. This I didn't want, so I set about minimising the risk, and the answers I got were that sleep is the best medicine and deep sleep at that. I confidently informed my neurologist that I was one of those fortunate people who could drink a double Espresso after a good evening meal and sleep like a baby. I can still picture his face as he informed me that I was a fool, and even if I thought I was asleep, I wasn't in a deep sleep and that this sleep wouldn't be doing me anything like the good that I needed. I swiftly changed my habits to no caffeine after 11am, which was just over two hours before my lunchtime sleep and monitoring my sleep, in order to track if anything was working or not working for me. I really believe that prioritising sleep and especially deep sleep, has been the firm foundation for the recovery from the brain injury. I think this has been aided along the way by keeping hydrated throughout the day and night and exercising sensibly.

One thing that I'm convinced has had a real benefit for me is a prayer I've prayed nearly every time I've gone to bed. When I'm lying down to sleep I've asked the Lord to fill me with his Holy Spirit and for that Spirit to wash through me and clear out everything in me that's not pleasing to Him; predominately any toxins in my brain and build up in my arteries. I've found it very comforting and the Lord sent the Holy Spirit to be a helper and to work with us. I think that by repeatedly praying this prayer and asking to be washed through by the Holy Spirit, has given me an increasing desire to be in a better and better relationship with the Lord. I'd like to think it's also cleansed my body from the toxins, but I don't really care about that because I trust that the Lord will keep me here on earth as long as He wants and when He calls me home, it's going to be so exciting.

SECOND CHANCE

I believe our responsibility in the church is to go to the world — a world so desperately in need of our product — and to tell them straight out what we have and why it meets the need they're longing to satisfy.

Chapter 11

Guy Rope 2 –
Unpaid Activities

"In everything I did, I showed you that by this kind of hard work we must help the weak, remembering the words the Lord Jesus Himself said: 'It is more blessed to give than to receive.'"

- Acts 20:35

These three guy ropes don't need to be exactly equal, but they need to be similar in positioning and strength. I think the unpaid activities, outside of the physical health exercise stuff, are important — not only to our own wellbeing, but to the society within which we live and are a part of. As we "develop" in the UK, there appears to be less communities where people spend their lives; cradle to grave, in the same location, with the same people around them. The ease of travel and communication has opened up the world, for the better I believe, but to the detriment of local community.

I think that the recent Covid pandemic highlighted the importance of community and maybe shook us a little into thinking about what we may have lost, but the general trend towards people being able to pursue their dreams further afield, also leads to more of a focus on what 'I' want and less on what 'we' need. I think there's a real benefit from strong local communities; places where people know their neighbours and work together to achieve things collectively. If we're not careful, the local communities that we still have will disappear, because it's easier to use a supermarket or shop online, than it is to support the village convenience store. It's easier to stay in, potentially alone, using social media and technology as the means of communicating with the outside world, rather than getting out and meeting people. I know that for some, such as the infirm, new technology can be a great benefit and I'm all for using new technology to the fullest (allowing us to get all the benefit it offers), but we must be careful that we don't lose things from our lives that we only recognise the value of once they're gone. Then it's probably going to be too late to get them back.

I've been very fortunate because we've been living in an Old Vicarage and have a lovely church as our next-door neighbour. Since becoming a Christian in the early nineties, I've tried to attend church every week, for fellowship with fellow believers. Since my cardiac arrest, having a little more free time and Sam wanting to get me out from under her feet, she persuaded me to take on the treasurer role of the church next door — St. John's, Norley part of the diocese of Chester. Wow! What an experience suddenly having my eyes opened to the workings of the church! I'd like to say opened, but it's more the slow clearing of the fog, partly due to how the Church of England (CofE) operates and partly due to my brain struggling to learn something new.

I'll give you my conclusion up front and it is that the CofE has so much potential, and so much to offer that it's exciting trying to help it achieve what I believe it should. I come at it with a business mindset and I know the CofE is not a business, but in my simple head, a business is an organisation that supplies a product to customers that want to buy it and generally that means understanding what benefits your product offers, understanding what your customers need and linking the two. If a business doesn't tell potential customers what they're selling, generally they won't make sales and if customers can't see or understand what a business is offering, they won't buy. The product also has to be fit for purpose.

The global Church is one church. We are the Body of Christ in the world and in our wisdom (and stupidity) we've split up and created divisions over what elements of doctrine we think are most important and created all sorts of different groups within. A simple example is Baptists, Methodists and Anglicans. I could go and google the differences, but I haven't because this isn't about emphasising the differences, but the common core, which is Jesus Christ. As the world falls into greater and greater uncertainty, apparent stress and injustice, this will inevitably lead to more conflict and acrimony.

With all of this going on around, the Church (of which the CofE is a significant part) is sitting on the answer to the problems in the world. We have what the world is desperate to buy, but rather than the world looking at our shop window and seeing Jesus, they look and either see acrimony, division or just a confused mess that they turn away from. We know the hope we have in Jesus Christ and this is what the world is looking for. From a business perspective, we have the product to offer, we have a market that is desperately looking for the product we have, but we appear unable to link the two. I believe our responsibility in the church is to go to the world — a world so desperately in need of our product — and to tell them straight out what we have and why it meets the need they're longing to satisfy. But we're not doing this. Rather, we're getting seduced by the world into trying to sell them what they say they're looking for. I think the key behind any successful business is for them to sell their product, by showing it to the market in the right light, and in a way that simply explains all the features and benefits. We're selling Christ crucified, for each and every human being in the world. We're not selling man-made buildings, meetings and organisational structures. We need to use these things to sell our product, which is Christ crucified, but not let the "other things" become our product. From a business perspective, we have the market reach, we have some level of prominence in virtually every city and village across our country. We need to get moving to give our neighbours the product that they're searching for, but recognise that they're a) not searching for it in our church buildings and b) they don't know what we have. So, unless we tell them clearly, they'll never know and we mustn't expect them to know. As every month goes by, I think the world knows gradually less and less about what Jesus' death and resurrection mean for them and they more and more associate "the church" with what they read and see in the news: division and man-made arguments.

This is one of the ways I've started to use what I call my "third guy rope" and I can feel a second book coming on already and it's only been a year since I took up the treasurer mantle.

The other way happened a bit by "accident" you'd say. I would say that the Lord's hand was in it and it might be sometime until we see where it's all leading, but it has been an amazing and uplifting experience. When Sam and I first moved up north, the business at that time, Texkimp Limited, was based at The Old Schoolhouse in Northwich. This was an old black and white primary school building along one of the main roads leading into Northwich. It was a great location, near Manchester and Liverpool, in easy reach of good airports and the UK motorway network. It was a short distance from North Wales and the Lake District and generally it's both a beautiful and convenient area to live in. It also worked well for a subcontract manufacturing business. As the business developed, we ran out of space and moved to a new site about a mile or so away and The Old Schoolhouse was then used for a recruitment arm that Cygnet Group was developing. Just after I had my incident, the recruitment business, Perpetual Engineering Partnerships Ltd., moved to premises in Knutsford and The Old Schoolhouse was left empty. I tried to sell it, but both times, for different reasons, the sales fell through at the last minute. I was really wondering what to do with the property with its small outside office, which we called "The Gatehouse" (it had two rooms, a kitchenette and a loo). It was becoming apparent that whilst Sam loved having me alive and around, it probably wasn't best for our marriage if I was at home permanently. While I thought I was being useful reorganising shelves, cupboards and the fridge, I'm not sure it was taken as positively as I expected it to be (which I found surprising as I was only trying to help her do everything better!). So, I was gently relocated to the Gatehouse for a portion of the week and was sitting looking at the empty main building, praying and wondering about it. I started talking to numerous interested charities about using it, with the deal that they paid no rent, but they were responsible for the annual costs of running it and maintaining it in the state it was in. It was about the time when Covid was starting and I received a call from David Briggs, the then Lord Lieutenant of Cheshire, who knew me from when we dropped the flag on his head (or he pulled it down; depending on which is the better story at the time) when Cygnet won the Queen's award for Export. David said that he felt that food was going to become an issue with Covid and that he'd like to introduce me to a charity called "Changing Lives Together" who weren't currently working with food, but who were planning to step in and help the food banks and others. We quickly did a deal and they're now not only well ensconced in The Old Schoolhouse, but have developed and are developing what they're doing to help people at a rapid rate. At the time of writing, they've just rebranded as the "The Very Green Grocery" and are having a significant impact in the local community.

But exciting as it is to see positive things being done to deal with local situations, challenges across the country have two distinct elements that stand out for me:

Firstly, the need right on my doorstep. I've worked at The Old Schoolhouse for over twenty years and it's been in the family for much longer. I've been shocked to find out what's going on, literally on my doorstep, a few hundred meters away. We have numerous people, often young single parents, living in accommodation where there are no cooking facilities. I had to ask about it, only to be told that it was because they found them to be a waste of valuable space; given that they didn't know how to cook and prepare food and would rather have another bedroom. So how were they eating? Well fast food was often the answer. Most of us know that this is an expensive way to live — it's not as healthy and therefore not ideal, but what I hadn't realised was that this was a real problem, on my doorstep, in leafy Cheshire. I might have believed it was a problem in the worst areas of our big cities, but this was happening in what appeared to be a reasonably well-off part of our country. It's not right, but what do we do? If the problem was easy to fix, it would've been fixed already, but this is a problem that I believe we can fix as a country, if we can all get behind it. It requires various different skills at different times and in different quantities, all working together to create a permanent fix and not a band aid. It's easy to try and get the government to carry the load, but I don't believe that this is the type of load that the government should be carrying or even try to carry.

Secondly, the positive impact it has on the volunteers — the people that give their time, energy, skills and experience to the problem and often doing jobs that the world would describe as "below" them. However, these would be jobs that need doing, so they do them with a smile and a laugh. It's amazing how much ability, good will and friendship there is in the world that we don't tap into and connect with. It's given me a real belief in the power of pulling people together, around a common cause or mission, to not only satisfy the common objective, but also bring great benefit to every part of the community.

The scariest thing about a brain injury is that you don't know what you don't know and nowhere was this more apparent than in the business world.

Chapter 12

Guy Rope 3 –
Paid Activities

"By the sweat of your brow you will eat your food until you return to the ground, since from it you were taken; for dust you are and to dust you will return."

- Genesis 3:19

Business. It's amazing — such a key part of my life and necessary for so many reasons! It's such a powerful element of life that it can, quite easily, get out of control. I believe we were originally made to work and the fall, when Adam and Eve got it so wrong, right at the beginning of time, made that work difficult and hard. My belief is that if we could properly work together, divide the spoils of work sensibly and allow everyone on the earth to play to their owns strengths, then what we have now would become a very pale comparison. We might see this in heaven. I can't wait to find out.

I'm sure I'm not alone here and work is probably the main area of life that I've wanted to include in this book but haven't been able to until now. It's easy to say words and to want to mean them, but deep down you know that they're not entirely true. It would've been the same for me and business. I knew that "work" was a guy rope to my life and I was, and am, totally happy with the concept that work plays this key but supporting part to my life. However, the reality is that I'd not only let business become so much more, but it had also grabbed me and entwined me far more than I cared to admit, or even wanted to deal with. Fortunately, the Lord wanted me to deal with it and being so gracious, He not only gave me time to process what was going on, but also provided the right people to walk alongside me at the right moments.

The scariest thing about a brain injury is that you don't know what you don't know and nowhere was this more apparent than in the business world. For me, this was like the two-sided coin analogy, where I had the wonderful benefit of owning a business that was able to provide for me and the family however, the other side to this coin is that I was too powerful. I had too much influence and the team in the business were used to me performing at a certain level and in a certain way. I was someone who knew exactly what I wanted to try and achieve and how to do it. I loved having the dreams for the future, going after these dreams fully, but being totally content to change my expectations as opportunities changed. I think I just assumed that everyone else was the same; really content with the dreams and an ever-changing landscape of opportunities. Some dreams continuing and others being left to wither and die. If only I'd known then what I know now, things would probably have been so different.

I was brought up in a business family. One of my earliest memories was of my bedroom at home in Knutsford, becoming "the office." I got moved upstairs to a room Dad was renovating and in my bedroom, there appeared things like an old metal filing cabinet, a desk and a drawing board. Dad was an engineer with the gift of being able to design and make things, from concept to final product using a wide variety of materials. He'd also had the opportunities of a good education and training at work, culminating in him being the Managing Director of my grandfather's, his father-in-law's business, WHK Products. William Harry Kimpton had built a business that made machines for processing fibres; predominately for the Lancashire cotton mills, during and after the war. At the end of the 1960s and start of the 1970s, business was challenging. They had a reasonably large workforce with a shop floor of several hundred and had the challenge of business at that period for the country. The world was opening up, ways of doing business were changing and businesses (to not only survive but also to grow and prosper), had to adapt and change. This is easy to say, however the reality of adapting to change for most businesses means that jobs change and therefore people need to change what they do. This is easy for some and much more difficult for others. I believe that work is something that everyone was made to do, but as a race (globally, nationally and regionally), we've got it wrong. I don't think that it's possible for us to do it "perfectly" and therefore our challenge is to do "work" with as little wrong as possible. I'll be coming back to this in a little bit.

My father had the challenge of keeping the business alive, keeping people employed when the market was rapidly shifting to other countries and the textile manufacturing industry was no longer globally competitive in this country. In a nutshell, this ended up with the business needing new owners to enable it to continue and ultimately a stand-off arose with the unions. In the end, it brought about the need for my bedroom to be turned into an office.

Mum and Dad, Janet and Colin Smith, set up TexKimp (the Tex from Textiles and Kimp from Kimpton) along with one of Dad's close friends from university, Alastair Barker, who was able to bring a willing pair of hands and a different perspective to the operation. They started with nothing and my sister, Kiersty and I were brought up from 1974 (when I was 7 and she was 4) with this fledgling business being a part of our daily lives. Home and business were totally intertwined. It was a fascinating upbringing and when you don't know anything else, you just accept what's going on. Tony Heap joined as a draughtsman and Ken Jones started working in the garage. Lunch was sitting around the kitchen table and that was life. We knew nothing else and inevitably absorbed how to do business without even realising it. One of Dad's key strategies was to never employ someone if he could sub-contract the work to someone else, at a fair price, with the right quality of supply and delivery. This allowed my parents to manage their fixed costs and commitments and initially this work was around the UK industrial areas that my father was familiar with. He relatively quickly teamed up with some individuals that he worked with previously who lived mainly in Europe, but also a few in the US and started selling our machines into the fibre markets that were developing around the world.

For all these early years we had a great childhood, with Mum and Dad around home much of the time, even if they were absorbed with the business. We knew that cash was tight and I can still remember walking around the supermarket in Knutsford, Mum, clicker in hand, sending me to put items back on the shelves when we'd reached our limit. It was just what we did and it was only later in life that I started to appreciate the decisions my parents had to make, with money being so tight. As kids, I don't think my sister and I ever really knew that it was so tight, because Mum and Dad just kept on going, being positive and working virtually every hour they could. Their example gave me such a strong foundation, both for cash management but also for marriage and partnership.

This book isn't the right forum to talk about the business learnings from the last seven years, apart from to say how much my head has changed and that my heart is still playing catch-up. I love business, all aspects of it, but particularly seeing what might be possible and then going after it. To me, business is all about people and the relationships you have with those people — whether they're your customers, your suppliers or your work colleagues. I believe that each of us has been created to work and most of us have been designed to work with other people. We each have different gifts and abilities and in order to be effective we need to bring our complementary skills together, to create something that works, something that functions properly and effectively. I love the whole jigsaw of putting the different pieces of business together, to create a whole that functions well. I'd love to say I did it perfectly, but I can now see that there were much better ways of doing most bits of it.

My key takeaways from being able to look back at my business, the business that I'd led for twenty years, but was looking back at dispassionately (as I could only remember the early days), was that I allowed myself to get too carried away and diverted into other interesting projects, to properly finish anything. The success was great, but it also meant that I and those around me could justify what we were doing, especially when we compared ourselves with other companies around us. I talk about comparison in chapter 15, but here it had the effect of allowing me to be satisfied with our performance and to stay focused on what I enjoyed most, which was getting out into the market and going after new opportunities. With the benefit of hindsight, I'd have had alongside me someone or a few people, who were very different from me in outlook and experience, but similar in desire and how we wanted to live our lives. I'd have made sure these individuals had the "power" to make me stop and listen. I now believe that the Lord was asking me to grow my business in a different way, but because it wasn't a way I was familiar with, I changed what the Lord told me, to fit what I knew. What I should've done, was find people with the experience and understanding that I didn't have, to build the business that the Lord was leading me to. Simply, He was telling me to create a group of businesses (ten was the number I settled on), where each business had its own managing director and leadership team and needed to stand on its own two feet but was also part of this group of businesses where they all worked together when there was common good to be gained. I loved the ideas, the new start-ups, but easily got bored with the details of how they were performing day to day. I too easily, and I believe wrongly, trusted people to just know what to do, because to me it seemed obvious. That was not only wrong, but it was poor leadership. My responsibility was to ensure that all my team, but especially my business leaders, had the necessary skills to be very successful in their roles. We did a lot right but fell down on ensuring the execution was properly carried out to completion.

So, for example, we had a business plan in May 2016, but when I "fell over" and was immediately taken out of the picture, the business plan that I thought there was full agreement on, suddenly had individuals pushing for what they'd been thinking previously, with me now out of the picture, rather than demonstrating that they were fully behind what I'd have claimed was our agreed plan. This was poor leadership on my account and I was responsible for ensuring that all of my senior team were behind and fully on board with the plan we were executing. But in reality, it would've been carried out by my force of personality and position of power, keeping everyone aligned.

It's also important to not let past failings and disappointments negatively affect our future goals and ambitions.

Chapter 13

Midway

"Do not conform any longer to the pattern of this world, but be transformed by the renewing of your mind. Then you will be able to test and approve what God's will is — His good, pleasing and perfect will."

- Romans 12:2

In my recovery journey, whilst it's been fantastic, it's also been the most frustrating, annoying time of my life. Sharing my emotions here on paper is very helpful for me and hopefully also for some of the readers of this book. However, I encourage you to dip in and out of this chapter as you see fit. Missing it entirely is more than acceptable.

I've ebbed and flowed in my emotions over the six years and can't yet decide to what level I'm able to recover and if it's even relevant, how it could be measured. I've just finished talking about perspective and appreciation (both of which are fantastic) and when I stop and properly take stock of my situation, I'm totally onboard with everything I've written about my learnings. However, the reality of life makes it much harder to do and to live than it is to write about it.

Crying out to God, as David did in his psalms, allows the grief and frustration to be expressed. In expressing it and giving it to God, hope for the future springs forth where God will restore, redeem and make all things new.

The ability to get to the place where I was abandoned to God, wasn't something I found I could do before. I was always clinging on to the "I," the "me," "my" way, "my" strength and "my" abilities. But in reality, it's all God's! I find that when I truly trust Him, He gives me back a freedom and peace about the future that's wonderful.

The world wants to snatch this peace away and the way it does that is insidious, but we need to be alerted, aware and prepared. A fall, even a stumble, often happens over something innocuous. Something insignificant like a small ruck in a rug can cause an old person to trip, fall and break a bone, potentially a hip or a shoulder, but enough to cause them to have to go into hospital. This will in turn get them out of their routine and incapacitates them to some extent for a number of weeks. However, this change in routine — the stopping of doing every day things such as walking upstairs — then makes it much harder to get back to those activities. It's possible, but only after much work, positive thinking and often with the need of encouragement. If that external encouragement isn't there, then this innocuous stumble becomes the life-altering event that can't be reversed. None of these events are ever planned. Rarely are we properly prepared, but they will happen to most of us, at some point. I touched on it earlier when I was talking about physical health in chapter 10, but managing ourselves to ensure we make the best of every moment of our lives is something that I think we rarely do. We can't see an immediate need and the effort isn't worth the sacrifice, whether that's time, effort, potentially money or a combination of all three. I was certainly in this category of not even thinking about it, and it nearly cost me my life.

Now my approach is to deal with both the long term and the short term at the same time.

I titled this chapter "Midway" and I'm not sure if it's because I think I'm midway through my recovery journey, or midway through my life (hopefully both are true). Assuming they are, that begs the question, "How should I live the rest of my life?" and I cover this in the final two chapters. However, this midway point is key, as this is the point when I'll set the direction of travel for the rest of my life. Inevitably that journey will have a different shape to the one I envisage now, but the direction I set off on and the destination I'm aiming for will be key. It's also important to not let past failings and disappointments negatively affect our future goals and ambitions. I'm convinced that we have so much to hope for and so much to be excited about, that we need to pro-actively ensure that we're consciously putting the past behind us; having learnt from all our experiences to the extent that they encourage us to be wiser and better moving forward. Injury or not, all off us at some point in our lives, reach a point where we need to set out how we want to live, what more we want to achieve etc. This midway point is often when parents become empty nesters, when we've paid off our mortgages and have some disposable income, when we retire or enter semi-retirement. These key events in life are happening earlier and earlier as a percentage of the time we have on earth. We're living longer and are generally healthier than our forefathers. When I was a kid, I remember somebody reaching eighty as being really old and having reached a significant milestone. There weren't many of their peers who reached that age (and that was in the late seventies, early eighties). Now it feels similar when someone reaches ninety and soon I believe it will be ninety-five and then one hundred. So we effectively reach this midpoint of our lives in our late forties and early fifties, hopefully having achieved a lot: a successful marriage, happy family of kids, great job, house, pension etc. Going into the next fifty, we should rightly expect to start faster than our first fifty and expect to end the second fifty slightly slower. But what are we going to achieve? What's life about? What's going to satisfy us and make us feel good?

To answer this, I come straight back to my tower. I believe our number one measure is the quality of the relationships we have and will have had. It's not about quantity, but about quality and ensuring that they're prioritised. We each have the ability to make the time we need, in order to have the relationship that the Lord wants us to have with Him. We need to do that and those of us that are married now have the time, especially with the kids leaving home, to properly look at our marriages. Talk with and listen to your spouse and together work out how you can each create the best marriage. However good it currently is, I don't believe we can ever stop investing in and improving our marriages. They'll all be different, but I believe that investing in your marriage is fundamental to the success of the second half of your lives. We've been joined, through marriage and become one and whilst the world outside might be doing everything possible to push down the importance of marriage, I believe that it's an institution created by our Lord, for our own benefit and the benefit of society as a whole. It's not for everyone and that's absolutely fine, but we should all work together to support those that are married to help each marriage be the best it can be. It's not surprising that something as important as marriage is currently coming under so much attack from many different quarters. My belief is that every single one of us, every human on earth, is ultimately going to be held accountable for how we lived our lives.

We're not responsible for how someone else lives, but we will be held responsible for what we allow to happen in our part of the world. This paradox can easily lead us to a) not stand up properly for what we believe and b) also truly love the person we're disagreeing with. I think that marriage is one of the fundamental building blocks, the foundation stone of the community we have in the world. Undermining these blocks will have far reaching consequences in years to come, combined with us not being able to rebuild anything as strong and long lasting.

If we look at the tower, now is when we can really allocate our time appropriately, using the three guy ropes to keep everything stable and balanced. While we work on having great relationships, we will do some amazing things both in paid work and other activities.

I'm writing this as the seventh anniversary of my cardiac arrest approaches and my ability to process data continues to strengthen. I'm still in need of help to achieve certain things (especially the appropriate understanding when I don't perform as anyone would wish — especially me). One of my New Year's resolutions has been to stop procrastinating and to become a true completer-finisher, hence the final publication of this book. It's not something I'd be able to achieve without the help of a few close friends who were keeping me accountable for agreed targets and who are a steady stream of quiet encouragement. Writing this book has forced me to go back over all the learnings of the past six or so years and it helped me to get clarity over what I'm looking to achieve in the rest of my life. No surprise there, but it all once again boils down to relationships. There's really no element of my life where getting the relationships right isn't the key to success — whether that be paid activities like Cygnet or unpaid activities like church, exercise and health. The success in every area will come down to how well I can handle and develop my relationships. I'd like to say that I'm an easy person, but I've come to the conclusion that I'm probably not quite as easy as I'd like to believe. I naturally think that this is a good thing, but if I'm going to have a successful next fifty years, I'm going to have to learn how to improve all my relationships. I find this an exciting challenge and I expect it to be one where everyone I speak to about relationships will have a fairly clear opinion as to what one should do. After all, most of us are looking for the right balance.

What excites me and gives me hope, are the opportunities all around me to make a difference. I've lost the desire, that's if I ever had it, to seek retirement but I have a real desire to live a long, healthy, fruitful life, until the Lord calls me home or returns. The "or returns" bit I've found personally really interesting and I have a reminder that pops up on my phone every morning with a verse from Luke's gospel chapter twelve from verse forty, "You also must be ready, because the Son of Man will come at an hour when you do not expect Him." What's interesting about this for me, is that this moment when the Son of Man comes, could be in more than a thousand years time, but it could also be tomorrow! We don't know and we're not expected to know, but we do know that it will be unexpected. Just like my cardiac arrest was unexpected, — totally unexpected. If we're not ready, it's going to be too late to get ready. We have been warned, it's absolutely fair, but we need to heed the warning and decide how we're going to live. So every day I naturally live to have as long a life as I can healthily have, being as productive as I can be, but with the daily awareness that everything I'm doing for future benefit could be pointless. Therefore, I need to be careful not to waste the enjoyment of the moment I have now. Even meeting the deadline to finish this book and park the desire to change it again.

I've found that getting into a few daily habits has been really good for creating a deep stability in my life.

Chapter 14

Measures and Comparisons

"It is better to be content with what little you have. Otherwise, you will always be struggling for more and that is like chasing the wind."

- Ecclesiastes 4:6

I think measures are really good. I personally love them and for many years have lived by the adage, "If you don't measure it, you can't improve it." I love numbers, knowing how fast I can do something, how something is measured and then being able to focus on that measure and change something (hopefully improving it) to get a better score.

In the last six years measures have really struck me as both dangerous and potentially damaging, along with being critical to living healthily. We're all very different as people. I believe this is an intentional part of the design that the Lord followed when He created us. He made us to work together, where we each play to each others' strengths and support each others' weaknesses, in order to arrive at the best outcome. I believe that heaven will be a place where we do this perfectly, where we're not selfish: not one person in heaven will have an ounce of selfishness in them, so there will be no need to "look after number one," because we'll all look after each other perfectly.

However, we're not in heaven yet, so until we get there, we have to live in the imperfect world that we all know,

hate. The Lord has been pushing me to keep my
ɳ me. I'm only writing this book now because I
d it's the right time for the readers to get it and I
woul. say the Lord pushed me with Matt Bird's "Writing
My Book Course," but what I've found is that it's also the
right time for me to be reminded of the amazing things
that have happened in my life over the last seven years.
The Lord's saying that He's given me my template for
living and that I'm not to be concerned with what
everyone else in the world is doing. My success in life is
being the best person that the Lord created me to be,
being the best version of me that I can possibly be and
your success is being the best person that you can
possibly be. We're all different, which is what makes the
world so special, but we have to make our measures
appropriate for what we're all trying to achieve (which is
surely for every single one of us on this earth, to be the
best person we can possibly be, with all the uniqueness
of our own gifts and challenges). This isn't anything to do
with other people, so measures can be
counterproductive, because they easily lead to
comparison with other humans. I'm not saying that
measures are bad, but I am saying that we need to be
very careful that when we compare ourselves to each
other, that we're ultimately trying to achieve an outcome
that benefits all of us individually and that benefits
society. Measuring ourselves is one way of identifying
who is strongest in which areas, thereby allowing us, as a
society, to play to our strengths. If we want something
heavy lifted up, then a stronger person is better for doing
this. If we want a message relayed quickly, then giving it
to the fastest runner is better than a slow runner, but the
line where we stop measuring and start 'just living' is
important.

We each have different strengths and weaknesses and we live in a society that ranks us by certain man-made measures. We're getting better at understanding the strength in our differences, at comparing ourselves positively, at knowing that differences are good and are part of what makes us stronger together.

I find that measuring how I'm performing every day and comparing my current performance with my past performance, can motivate me to try and be better and better. I've found that getting into a few daily habits has been really good for creating a deep stability in my life and I'd recommend the following to anyone who is debating where and how to start sorting their life out:

These four daily habits will help move you from overwhelmed to overflowing. I can't remember where I took them from, but I picked them up early in my recovery and I've found that keeping to them and not trying to make them better or different, has been really beneficial. So, if you're not sure what to do, pick these up, keep it simple and seek the Lord. He'll meet you where you are and help you to walk with Him alongside.

1. **Stay connected to Jesus every day.** *"I am the vine, and you are the branches. If you stay joined to Me, and I stay joined to you, then you will produce lots of fruit. But you cannot do anything without Me"* (John 15:5 CEV). If you try to go through life in your own power, you're going to be overwhelmed. You cannot fulfil your purpose and enjoy God's goodness unless you're plugged in to His power.

2. **Replace your complaining with gratitude.** *"Do everything without complaining and arguing"* (Philippians 2:14 NLT). Complaining is a deeply unhealthy emotion. On the other hand, studies have shown that gratitude is the healthiest emotion — it produces serotonin, dopamine and oxytocin in your brain; those are the chemicals that boost happiness and lower stress.

3. **Stop being stingy, and start being generous.** *"Bring the full amount of your tithes to the Temple, so that there will be plenty of food there. Put Me to the test and you will see that I will open the windows of heaven and pour out on you in abundance all kinds of good things"* (Malachi 3:10 GNT). God wired a universal law into the world: The more you give away, the more you're going to get. God did that because He wants you to become more like Him — and He is a giver.

4. **Stop comparing and start being content.** *"It is better to be content with what little you have. Otherwise, you will always be struggling for more, and that is like chasing the wind"* (Ecclesiastes 4:6 NCV). Contentment doesn't mean you don't have any goals, dreams or plans for your life. It simply means you don't need more in order to be happy.

By nature, people are discontent. But by God's grace, you can rest contently in His goodness to you. When you grasp that most things in your life are simply gracious gifts from God, your life will go from overwhelming to overflowing with God's abundance.

SECOND CHANCE

Keeping our minds in the right condition is absolutely fundamental and not just something we should take for granted. How you live now, at whatever age you currently are at, will affect your ability to make the most of your remaining years.

Chapter 15
Whose Way?
Those Final Years – 5 or 50?

*"No discipline seems pleasant at the time, but painful.
Later on, however, it produces a harvest of righteousness
and peace for those who have been trained by it."*

- Hebrews 12:11

Whatever we have left of our lives, the joy of living our remaining days well is so important to all of us. If you're reading this and feeling all positive and excited about the future, your future, then fantastic! Go and make the most of everything you can. However if you're reading this and feeling really down and depressed about what you believe your future holds, don't, and I'll explain why I can so confidently say this. If you read on from here, please make sure you read to the end of this chapter, as I'm about to start with a fairly depressing situation I went through.

We were on a family holiday in Cuba. It was fairly early on in my recovery and Sam had organised, with all the kids, that we should go somewhere special. Cuba was great. We spent a few days in Havana at the end of the holiday and one early evening, we came back to the hotel and all I remember was that it felt like chaos. A tour bus had just arrived, the lobby and reception were full of people, there was noise and activity everywhere and we, as a small family group, were undecided as to exactly what we were going to do, where we were going to go, when etc. I'd be surprised if you can't remember similar situations in your own lives and whilst it's frustrating, it's nothing special. However, I just couldn't cope. I felt nobody was making sense, nobody was listening to me, there was nobody in charge of what was going on and this created in me, a deep bubbling feeling of "unease" (probably the best way to describe it). It wasn't anger, nor frustration, but it was really deep in me and felt powerful. I took the elevator up towards our room and when I exited on our floor near the top, I sat down just outside the elevator and was able to look over an internal balcony down into the atrium, where all this "chaos" was going on. The only way I could see to get the attention I wanted, was to jump over the railing into the middle of the atrium. It sounds stupid as I write it, but I can vividly remember the emotions and feelings churning through my body and head and the lack of logic about what I felt I had to do. It was both weird and totally understandable at the same time. It was my tower that saved me. As I approached the railing, I knew that it wouldn't be pleasing to the Lord if I jumped and fortunately the simplicity around what I could and couldn't do, made it a clear no to jumping. I sat down and contemplated everything and slowly brought everything back into the right perspective, but it gave me an appreciation of how fragile our minds can be, and how much care we need to take of them.

What can appear so completely stupid when your mind is dealing with things properly, can seem like your only option when it's all going crazy. Keeping our minds in the right condition is absolutely fundamental and not just something we should take for granted. How you live now, at whatever age you currently are at, will affect your ability to make the most of your remaining years. Couple this with taking care of our bodies, then we're starting on a good footing. I'm now exercising physically at a sensible level for my heart, managing my diet and my weight and continuing to work at cleansing my brain. All of these activities are more pleasurable and I believe effective, with the relationships I have around each one.

My paid work, Cygnet Group, is an activity I'd like to be involved in until my dying day, with the condition that I'm only involved if I'm adding value. So getting myself mentally sharp and maintaining this brain function will be key, but the primary driver for me, is not generating income, which whilst important is not life critical. The primary driver is because I believe we've been made to work and that as a society we need to learn to appropriately keep everyone involved until their last few days. I think it's good for all of us, physically and mentally, but only if we do it appropriately. If we, as a society, could work out how to get the best from the older members of society, their learning and wisdom, without getting the bad bits that come with ageing and couple this with the energy, enthusiasm and drive for new ideas and ways of functioning of the younger members, we would all be better off. However, this will only happen if we collectively work differently, do our working hours differently, our remuneration systems differently and within reason treat each person as the unique individual, with their unique personal needs and gifts, as each of us deserves to be treated. In the last chapter we touched on comparisons and in the workplace I believe it's key that we don't compare how each of us is individually being involved, but we ensure that each person is giving and getting a fair deal. I had the pleasure and privilege of working with my parents and whilst it might have been more torturous for them than me, we were a close family that communicated well and had the strength of relationship to really work together well. I believe that they both benefited from being properly involved with the business into their later years. Both only properly stepped away due to the combination of my accident and Covid and are functioning really well in their eighties.

My unpaid activities centre around my work with the local church and through the charity using the Old Schoolhouse. The church that I'm a member of, I believe, can have such a fantastic positive impact on society. We have the most amazing hope and the infrastructure to reach all across society and that's just the human side, never mind what our Lord can bring. I think that the church has the potential to harness much more of what it has available and is responsible for and create some amazing, long-lasting good. I know it's not a business, but when I bring a business head and look at the potential of the assets and the people that it has within its organisation, I desperately want to help. If I can, I'd love to see this released to the benefit of the whole world. I believe this is what our Lord wants, but if we want to bring this change about, we have to do things differently; we have to change and understand that this is a key part of the journey. How we all work together, to bring our different gifts to the table, is the fun part of the challenge. But I fear that the obstacles currently impeding change will be very hard to either knock down or circumvent. I, for one, am not sure yet whether I've got enough in my tank to take on my part of this fight, but at least I know that the Lord will provide, if it's something He wants me involved in.

Life's all about relationships and making every relationship we have as special as it possibly can be, it's definitely quality before quantity and whilst our marriages and family life is absolutely fundamental, the relationship we each have, or don't have, with our Lord is our top priority.

So I leave you with your thoughts about the excitement of the future, with the wonderful combination of the "certain" and "uncertain" bits. I encourage you all to "make your choice" and make it now if you haven't already.

Was Jesus really God's Son, born of a virgin, who lived a sinless life and was crucified to pay for your sins, in order for a perfect God to be able to forgive you and welcome you into an eternity in heaven with Him?

Will our Lord be waiting to greet you with the words, *"Well done, good and faithful servant! You have been faithful with a few things; I will put you in charge of many."* - Matthew 25

Everyone has made a choice and it's either been made consciously or unconsciously and it's saying either "yes" or "no." There's no in-between — death could come to any of us, at any moment or Jesus could return in the next minute (see Luke 12:40). Don't be caught out because you've bought into the devil's lies and waited to make a decision. You're either "in" or you're "out." If you're procrastinating and aren't sure then you're not in, so you must be out. Everyone can be in, by accepting that Jesus died for them on that cross at Calvary.

I look forward to meeting you in heaven. The Lord already knows you intimately and He wants to be in a personal relationship with you today.

About the Author

Matthew Kimpton-Smith is married to Sam and they have four children: Max 28 and married to Naomi, Claudia 26, Antonia 17 and Harry 13. They live in Cheshire, UK, near where Matthew was brought up. They head up a family business, Cygnet Group Ltd.

Matthew was educated at Shrewsbury School and then read Economics at Cambridge, before qualifying as a chartered accountant with Price Waterhouse, London in the early nineties.

Matthew rowed at school and university, competing in the Oxford and Cambridge boat race in 1988 and 1989, along with U18 and U23 representation for Great Britain.

Matthew gave his life to Christ in 1991, after attending an Alpha course at HtB.

He joined his parents in their business, Texkimp, in the mid-90's and found his true vocation, leading a small group of people, in a business, to achieve great things globally.

About PublishU

PublishU is transforming the world of publishing.

PublishU has developed a new and unique approach to publishing books, offering a three-step guided journey to becoming a globally published author!

We enable hundreds of people a year to write their book within 100-days, publish their book in 100-days and launch their book over 100-days to impact tens of thousands of people worldwide.

The journey is transformative, one author said,

"I never thought I would be able to write a book, let alone in 100 days... now I'm asking myself what else have I told myself that can't be done that actually can?'"

To find out more visit
www.PublishU.com

30.22 Breakfast?
162.40 Supermarket.
16.88 Pharmacy.
4.65 Snacks.
54.72 parking
5.21 Glasses holder.
14.88 Food.
→ 10.94 Food.
21.71 Restaurant drinks.
155.46 Christmas Eve dinner
126.97 Intersport.
26.73 Food.
26.06 Olympic spot - shin protectors
5.48 Supermarket
~~13.46~~) ~~Food~~ Drinks
13.46 } (La Ratrah)
~~13.46~~)

                        17.15 cross
13.05 Fuel?   17.58 Drinks
10.27 Drinks
23.71 ATM.
3.14 Groceries
17.26 ~~Food~~. Drinks.
103.30 Meal out

914.57
1,250.00
_____
2,164.57

10-17 June Scotland.
Canada.
Galapagos.

3-15 May Africa?
72   Sky   23 Aug - 8 Sept Canada/US
64   Compassion   19-22 Sept Fez. (OSMA)
400   Greyfriars   28 Dec - 2 Jan Marrakech.
35   Mark Ridley   or
                     21 Dec - 4 Jan Cape
84.59 Zurich   Town?

17.00 Tom / Spotify

27.69 Travel insurance

9.01 Specsavers.

236.56 Animal Life.

(52 × 4) Julie.   - Hotel.
208.00 ——→   - Fuel
                         - Food
1,153.84. __   - Hostels

                         £ 1,010.67
                           854.99
                         _____
£835.66   1,865.66

17.58 - Burg - Breakfast cffe.
17.10 - croissant
103.86 Shell.
3.83
23.76
6.09
2.00 } cffee
2.00
6.83 . family supper
161.80 Le Vosco - supper
73.81 Breakfast + tax.
34.77 Duty free (Travis)
30.00 petrol.

Printed in Great Britain
by Amazon